Managing Your Marketing Career

The Marketing Series is one of the most comprehensive collections of books in marketing and sales available from the UK today.

Published by Butterworth-Heinemann on behalf of the Chartered Institute of Marketing, the series is divided into three distinct groups: *Student* (fulfilling the needs of those taking the Institute's certificate and diploma qualifications); *Professional Development* (for those on formal or self-study vocational training programmes); and *Practitioner* (presented in a more informal, motivating and highly practical manner for the busy marketer).

Formed in 1911, the Chartered Institute of Marketing is now the largest professional marketing management body in Europe with over 22,000 members and 25,000 students located worldwide. Its primary objectives are focused on the development of awareness and understanding of marketing throughout UK industry and commerce and on the raising of standards of professionalism in the education, training and practice of this key business discipline.

Books in the series

Managing Your Marketing Career

ANDREW CROFTS

Published on behalf of
the Chartered Institute of Marketing

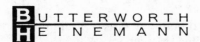

Butterworth-Heinemann Ltd
Linacre House, Jordan Hill, Oxford OX2 8DP

 PART OF REED INTERNATIONAL BOOKS

OXFORD   LONDON   BOSTON
MUNICH   NEW DELHI   SINGAPORE   SYDNEY
TOKYO   TORONTO   WELLINGTON

First published 1991

© Butterworth-Heinemann Ltd 1991

All rights reserved. No part of this publication
may be reproduced in any material form (including
photocopying or storing in any medium by electronic
means and whether or not transiently or incidentally
to some other use of this publication) without the
written permission of the copyright holder except in
accordance with the provisions of the Copyright,
Designs and Patents Act 1988 or under the terms of a
licence issued by the Copyright Licensing Agency Ltd,
90 Tottenham Court Road, London, England W1P 9HE.
Applications for the copyright holder's written permission
to reproduce any part of this publication should be addressed
to the publishers.

British Library Cataloguing in Publication Data
Crofts, Andrew
  Managing your marketing career.
  I. Title
  658.80023

ISBN 0 7506 0152 3

Photoset, printed and bound in Great Britain by
Redwood Press Limited, Melksham, Wiltshire

Contents

Foreword

The hardest and most important task for any company is to attract the right calibre of employee. Twenty or thirty years ago many big companies believed that the best way to do that was to offer security and the opportunity for a 'cradle-to-grave' career within one organization.

Things are now different. The pace of change has quickened enormously and companies evolve very much more quickly. Requirements, therefore, for people and skills change too. At the same time employees are much more anxious to control their own careers and to change companies to gain experience and to develop their careers more quickly. There is a growing realization that anyone who wants to be successful must make their own plans and must know what the market requires of them.

This change in attitude also has advantages for the employers since employees who are in control of their lives and careers are probably more in control of their jobs as well.

I very much welcome the approach taken in this book. It provides a welcome sign that change in attitudes is well underway. From my own experience little real advice is available to people in planning their careers, particularly in marketing and selling. I started my own career as a salesman and took the then Institute of Marketing and Sales Management exams in the evenings as part of a postal study course. On gaining the Institute's Diploma I decided later to move into marketing and specifically into product management. I have found many of the skills developed both in the selling and marketing phases of my career have proved extremely valuable when moving into general management.

I hope that this book will provide a useful guide through the careers jungle for anyone who is ambitious and far sighted enough to be aiming to get to the top in marketing. I wish it had been available earlier.

Peter J. Davis
Chairman and Chief Executive,
Reed International

Introduction: What is marketing?

Even today there is still a degree of confusion as to what marketing actually is. The Chartered Institute of Marketing defines it as 'the management process responsible for identifying, anticipating and satisfying customer requirements profitably'.

What it is not is selling, although selling is a vital component of marketing. Marketing thinking and planning begins at, or even before, the drawing board and ends only when the company has made certain that the customer is really satisfied with the product or service provided.

It is a business function which endeavours to bring the right goods and services to the customer in a profitable way. It is an essential activity and it provides wide scope for people with qualifications in technical, arts and science subjects.

The three broadest categories into which marketing falls are consumer, industrial and services. The consumer end of the spectrum, including all the domestic products and foodstuffs sold through the major retail outlets, tends to be the most sophisticated in terms of marketing, simply because the companies involved have been practising it for the longest, but there are exciting opportunities to be had in all the sectors.

Those who succeed in marketing have the satisfaction of seeing their activities and decisions genuinely affecting the success of their company. They enjoy the challenge of dealing with a rapidly changing business environment, and of constantly trying to provide a better product or service to satisfy customer demand. They are also well rewarded for their achievements.

Within the marketing profession there are a number of disciplines. Anyone hoping to get to the top of the general management tree from a start in marketing will need to be familiar with all of these and skilled in some. Each of the disciplines, however, offers career opportunities for those who want to specialize.

There is market research, product development, planning, pricing, packaging, promotion (which includes advertising, sales promotion, direct marketing, merchandising and public relations), sales, distribution, overseas operations and exporting, and after-sales service.

Marketing is all about team effort and marketing management is about providing basic information and guidance on prospective markets, their behaviour, size and potential for each product or service within the company. Management's role is to promote better marketing throughout the company structure, to draw up marketing plans and to ensure that these are implemented efficiently and profitably.

Marketing starts with the evaluation of customer needs and wants, and goes on to embrace the design of the product, the branding and packaging, the time for test marketing and national launch, the advertising and promotional back-up, delivery and after sales services. It is also about communication between the various disciplines involved in the corporate process.

1 Controlling your own career

For the majority of management workers the idea of controlling your own career is relatively new. Until recently this was a luxury limited to the rich and the entrepreneurial. Since the Industrial Revolution most people have grown up with the idea of companies employing them, perhaps for the whole of their working lives, and of living in fear of displeasing their bosses and causing the companies to dispense with their services. That situation is now changing; the powerbase is shifting in favour of the individual, particularly the skilled managerial worker.

A concept of corporate loyalty is vital to any successful company, but the companies that are successful in generating it are the ones that provide the right career mixes for their people. A company that expects loyalty from its workforce simply in exchange for giving them employment is likely to be disappointed. Good players can now choose which teams they give their loyalty to, and they expect to be rewarded in a variety of different ways. One of the rewards they will demand is the right to be the masters of their own destinies.

This sort of respect for the abilities of the individual has long been accepted in the professions. People will travel a long way to hire the services of a good doctor, lawyer or accountant. Good marketeers are also now coming into demand, with companies realizing that without their services they will fail to grow and prosper.

Skilled managers who can operate effectively in the modern world are hard to find and even harder to keep. They are going to become scarcer as the effects of the much talked about 'demographic timebomb' begin to be felt. The onus is on companies to make themselves attractive to the best people. All you as an individual have to do is ensure that you make yourself the best, and then plan how you can get the most beneficial deals from the companies offering you employment.

You have, in other words, got to 'market yourself'. You must work out what your USP is, what your potential employment market is, and what price you are going to be able to get for your services. You need to have strategic plans, and you need to think of your image, packaging, presentation, advertising and public relations along the way.

Members of the managerial working population are now in a stronger position than ever before to shape and control their individual destinies. At the same time the great companies have proved that they are not on the whole to be entrusted with anything as important as a person's entire career. You may find that market forces or political expediency have led to you losing your job when you are only half-way through your climb, even though you had always imagined yourself staying with one company for life. There are, of course, many people who do stay with their original employers perfectly happily, but anyone who does not have a plan for how they will survive if things go wrong is laying themselves open to disaster.

If your employers want to keep you from cradle to grave then they must make sure that they can give you the satisfactions that you want, not the ones that they think you should have. There are still companies who can maintain the loyalty of their employees from the beginning to the end of their careers, but they can't automatically expect to do so, they have to work at it.

You the individual also have to ensure that they know what it is you want to achieve, and that the company is constantly reminded of the need to move you on to the next stage. If it forgets about you and allows you to waste your talents and become demotivated it will be the company's loss, but also yours and you could waste a lot of time waiting for a break to come when you could have gone up and asked for it years before.

Whereas once we might have thought that any company of size would be there forever, we now know that even giant companies can come and go almost overnight in the world of takeovers, mergers, de-mergers and changing market trends. No longer can any employer take someone on at eighteen and guarantee to look after them until they die. Within a span of forty years a company could have entirely changed its make-up and style of working. We have all seen how quickly people are laid off when firms hit hard times, or how new managers move in to tighten up the ship and sweep out all that has gone before. You may think that couldn't happen to your company, but supposing they merged with another firm and your job was the same as another person's in the other company? If there are two people and there is only one job, that means you stand a 50 per cent chance of ending up on the street, however good you are. No one can guarantee your safety except you.

On top of this there are the changing skills needs and changing market needs. Just because the skill you have today is in demand now, that doesn't mean it will still be needed in ten or twenty years time. People are having to change and evolve all the time in order to keep up with the changes in technology and business life. In a perfect company the employers will make sure their people keep up with the times, but in an imperfect world they won't always have time to do that, so the responsibility falls on the individual.

The chances are that there is not a 'perfect job' waiting for you out there somewhere. If you wait for that to come along you may be out of work for a long time. You are versatile enough to be able to tackle any number of variations on a basic theme; there are many worthwhile jobs you could do which would give you what you need from employment. The more research you do into the different disciplines and sectors, the more options you will discover are possible and the greatest problem may be choosing in which direction to go. You may even decide that you are more suited to the world of self-employment.

The loyalty shown by previous generations to their employers has been seen too often to have been misplaced, and their trust betrayed. Companies now have to earn the loyalty of their people, and you have to be prepared to be betrayed at any time, and to know what actions you will take in these circumstances.

Whereas once dutiful employees might have felt grateful to an employer for taking them on, thus saving them and their families from the poorhouse, the boot is now very much on the other foot. Good managers are in short supply and companies can't survive in an increasingly competitive world without them.

There are plenty of people out in the marketplace, but very few of them are of the highest quality. This means that there is an enormous potential marketplace for anyone who equips themselves well for the race to the top, and who ensures that they can provide their employers with a really good product.

Individuals who market themselves effectively are in a position to pick and choose who they will work for and for how long. Employers now have to work hard in order to woo and keep their best people, and someone who knows what they want and where they are going can actually employ companies that suit their career needs at any one time rather than the other way round.

Instead of joining a business and then having to trust that your merits will be recognized and rewarded, you can now set out with a definite goal in mind, and search out the employers who will offer you the best way to reach that goal. Once inside a company you no longer have to keep quiet and do what you are told. If you are offered a sideways promotion which you are not sure about, for instance, you can take time to think about it and analyse what it will mean to your long-term prospects. If it is not in your career interests you can turn it down. If the company then tries to bully you into changing your mind, you will know that it is time to start looking around for another employer.

Ideally, however, you will be able to be entirely proactive in running your career, and it will be you who is suggesting what moves you would like to make and when you would like to make them, before the company has even thought of them. In this book we are setting out to demonstrate what some of the best moves might be, and also some of the worst. Every individual has different needs and is involved in different circumstances, but the general rules will apply to most people most of the time, and will serve to start the reader thinking of ways in which other people's experiences can be adapted to suit his or her particular needs.

Your job may belong to your employer, but your career belongs to you. You will need to succeed in the jobs that you agree to take on in order to reach your personal career goals, but the jobs must never be seen as ends in themselves, they are merely steps in a long-term ladder. You need to be able to develop a strategic sense about yourself in just the same way as you need a strategic sense about your company and your business. That means having long-term goals and a series of short-term plans on how to achieve them. You need to make yourself marketable at every stage of the way.

Executives who are looking after their own interests will also, in many cases, function better as team members. Because they have vested interests in being part of a successful operation, they are going to be doing everything they can to make sure that targets are achieved by everyone around them. Because they know that they can always move on to other places, they are likely to be more positive and less defensive in their attitudes to colleagues. It is vital to them that they build reputations for being good corporate citizens. If they leave a trail of disappointment and bad feeling behind them they will soon be unable to get new jobs because they will have no one to provide references, and their shortcomings will begin to show up on their CVs.

Someone who is building for the long term will even leave a company with order and foresight. Instead of just handing in their notice and going when something better offers, they will warn their employers that they are going to be looking for something else well in advance, and will help to make the hand-over to their replacement as smooth as possible. Once someone has realized that they are unlikely to reach the next stage of their career plan with their current employer, they can go to their bosses and warn them that they intend to leave in eighteen months' time, although they are open to be dissuaded should the company be able to offer them something worth staying for. This gives everyone plenty of time either to dissuade the mover from going, or to prepare for the departure to be as smooth as possible.

Setting the goals

No one expects someone of twenty to know where they want to be at fifty – although people who do have that far-reaching a goal are highly likely to succeed in achieving it – but anyone who is setting out to plan and control a career should be able to see at least ten or fifteen years ahead. If you don't know where you are going, there will be no way to tell whether you are on the right route or whether you are turning up blind alleys.

In order to identify the goals, you may need to give them signposts and labels. You may, in other words, need to resort to titles in order to judge how well you are doing. You might decide, for instance, to be a brand manager by twenty-five or a marketing director by thirty. Always remember that boxes and labels may be useful for identifying stages of a career, but they are not as important as the overall quality of the individual.

If you are planning on enjoying a long career it is more important that you are doing the right things to improve your skills and provide proof of your ability to achieve results than to build up a list of smart-looking titles. It's no good being a brand manager with no international or general management experience if you are hoping to reach the top in a major company. It would be better to be working on the ground for a few years in another country with a less impressive title but with the opportunity of getting some solid management experience and overcoming some genuine difficulties and problems. It is easy to be seduced by status symbols like titles, bigger offices and cars, when in fact you should be looking for the hardest and least rewarded tasks, because those are the ones that will show what you are made of.

Planning and luck

The only way to ensure success in any project is to plan. There are some people who will swear that they have reached the top through luck and through being in the right place at the right time. They are probably trying to make their rise to eminence appear more graceful and effortless than it in fact was. The chances are that they have kept a very careful map in their heads of where they are going, and have made all the right moves along the way to ensure that they are in as many potential right places as possible.

Only by continually putting yourself in the way of good fortune do you get lucky, and when luck does strike you have to have done the groundwork and have prepared the plans in order to recognize it and be able to take advantage of it.

This doesn't mean that you have to spend your life involved in political schemes and plots to survive and prosper in the corporate jungle; it merely means that you need to have a fixed course in your mind and that every so often you must stop to check that you are still heading in the right direction, so that you can make corrections if you are blowing off course.

Look upon your career as a vessel ploughing across a treacherous and stormy sea. Before you set out on the journey you must have a map, and then you will need a radar system to check where you are going. Every so often you will become preoccupied with surviving some particular storm, or dealing with a fire on board. Once the period of high activity is over, however, you can go back to the radar screen and check that you are still on course. If you find you have strayed you can then steer yourself back. If you continue fighting fires and ignoring the radar it is unlikely that you will reach your destination. Most people spend their lives fighting fires.

As you go along you need to pick up the right sort of experience to carry you on to the next stage of your journey, and you need to check your progress regularly: are you still travelling in the right direction, or have you allowed yourself to be diverted? Are your original goals still valid or have they proved to be unsuitable or unduly modest with time? Should you be changing course or adapting your goals to suit the changing circumstances?

There is no reason why you can't change your plans as you go along: being flexible and able to adapt to new circumstances is one of the prerequisites of success – the important thing is always to be in control. If things are not going as well as you would like, or you are not happy in your work, the remedy will be in your hands, you cannot wait and hope that someone else will put things right for you. In order to take the right remedial action, however, you need to know what the options are and how you can exercise them.

We all change as we grow up; someone of twenty will have very different ideas about what they want from life to someone of forty or fifty, but from the beginning there must still be a plan to work to.

In this book we are looking at most of the scenarios that are likely to confront a successful manager who chooses to enter the marketing profession; we are looking at some of the choices that confront professional marketeers during their careers; and we are suggesting what might happen if they choose one course of action or another.

There is no 'right way' to get to the top in marketing, but there are a number of wrong ways, decisions and choices that will almost inevitably set someone back in their career, or possibly stop them dead in their tracks. We have tried to identify these danger areas, and to suggest what steps someone facing one of these obstacles should take to avoid it. If you have already fallen into one of these traps, it is never too late, and we would hope that we can point you towards some ladders of escape that you haven't previously noticed.

The structure of the book follows, approximately, the structure of a typical marketeer's career. Certain choices are likely to arise at key points of a career, from the ones you make when leaving school or university, to the ones facing you at around forty when most people are reaching the peaks of their achievements and are looking for ways to capitalize on their past experience.

If nothing else, we hope that the book will stimulate you into asking yourself a number of key questions.

What is it that I want to achieve with my career?

What are my strengths and what are my weaknesses?

Given those, what are the options open to me?

What should I be doing today to ensure that I keep those options open for as long as possible?

What skills am I likely to need to be successful in the future?

Where are the best places to gain these skills?

Am I on a continuous learning curve, or am I standing still?

What new skills are emerging in the marketplace that I should learn about?

What new professional qualifications are becoming available to me?

What things could go wrong for me in the future?

How do I minimize the chances of those things happening?

If they do happen, what contingency plans do I have?

The fast track or the high road?

'Fast track' is a term with which most people are familiar, and which they associate with the idea of being successful. In fact it might be better to think of your progress through your career as a high road. A fast track suggests going too far too fast, cutting corners, taking unacceptable risks and possibly burning yourself out before you have reached your goal.

The fast track is a rather old-fashioned concept, imported from America, of single-minded career people who keep the blinkers on as they head for the boardroom, working eighteen hours a day and sacrificing everything at the altar of success. It is based on a system where there are unlimited human resources available, and Europe can no longer afford to think that. The word 'fast' suggests a lack of caution and deliberation, both of which are needed if you are hoping to climb to the top.

While there are those for whom workaholism is an enjoyable lifestyle, the majority of people who are truly successful throughout their lives manage to achieve a better balance. They serve the right apprenticeships in the right places, building a firm base of experience to help them make the right decisions later on. These people also balance their careers with their home lives, pacing themselves to run a marathon rather than a short, sharp dash. They even plan what they will do with their 'third age', the period after they have retired from what we traditionally think of as their 'working lives', a period in which they can actually produce the greatest achievements yet.

The dangers of the fast track are as great for the individual as for the employing company. If you move too fast you may get ahead of your own abilities, like a child which has outgrown its peer group and so gets put into a football team with much older children who have far more strength, stamina and experience. If you don't learn how to handle problems while you are on the way up, you are more likely to get into trouble later on. The fast track leads to people getting fired younger and younger, and industry ends up paying more for less at every level, leading to a volatility which in most sectors is undesirable.

However, those who feel that they are more temperamentally suited to the fast track will find all the necessary steps in this book as well. They will merely have to accelerate the timescales and perhaps miss one or two of the stages as they go along. They too may be successful, although it is unlikely that they will be able to maintain any success for as long as the people who stay firmly on the high road. They are also much more likely to shoot off the track, their wheels spinning in the air, to burst into flames in the stands.

2 A route to the top

There are two main reasons why someone might choose to pursue a career in marketing. Firstly it is a challenging and exciting profession, offering variety, scope, colour and the possibility of power. Secondly, and for some people more importantly, it can provide a ticket to top management.

This has not always been the case, and in the UK it is still less the case than in America, with some British companies not even having their marketing departments represented on their boards; but things are changing.

Both ICL and British Telecom were companies that ran into trouble at the beginning of the 1980s. When their problems were analysed it was seen that they were not paying enough attention to marketing. In fact they were paying it no attention at all. As a result they turned their attitudes around. British Telecom went out recruiting in a big way, and ICL decided to turn its existing workforce into a marketing-oriented company.

The ICL approach was interesting, and gives an idea of the way in which other companies in the future are likely to go. They now have a marketing team of some 700 people, who have been drawn from the company's workforce and given intensive training, firstly to understand the concepts, secondly to be able to practise the skills tactically, and thirdly to be able to plan strategically with them.

The results have been dramatic with both companies, but most noticeably with ICL because as a company it was more able to adapt to new thinking, and because the idea of marketing as the most important aspect of any business was entrenched in the top management.

Although the high technology industry has a long way to go before it catches up with the fmcg sector in marketing skills, ICL has set an example from which many other companies are attempting to learn. By tackling all the training internally ICL have been able to build a virtual business school of their own, and to change the whole way in which the company views its business. There are still many organizations that have not yet reached this stage of thinking. It may be that they have not yet reached the edge of the precipice and realized that they will have to jump or perish. It may be that there are not yet enough marketing people high enough in the company to be able to start the process off. Whatever the reason, it seems unlikely that they will be able to continue to ignore marketing for much longer.

The ICL story

The information technology industry is the most dynamic there has ever been, with new products and services appearing daily, many of which revolutionize their sectors of the market. The range of technologies, the variety of competitors, the changing market structures and developing client profiles all alter at varying rates. In 1981 ICL saw a loss of £50 million against a turnover of £711 million, and realized that its product/market portfolio no longer reflected the new market requirements. It was decided that the company needed to be restructured to reflect a new mission statement and the means of achieving the objectives that would support it.

The company decided to fund an extensive training and development programme which would eventually cover all areas of activity, including management, sales, quality, manufacturing, technical, customer service, development and marketing.

The mission for the team that was set the task of 'creative marketing' was to develop a skills base that would be equal to the best examples of industrial marketing in the world. This was to be achieved in a corporation that, at the time, had no common marketing language, little professional practice, no marketing process and a limited amount of marketing expertise.

It was felt that an appropriate marketing community would need to cover seventy countries, with departments requiring skilled resources ranging from a few people to hundreds. Their educational levels might range from the equivalent of GCSE through to PhD, while the markets they addressed would not only vary in structure and type from country to country, but would also contain varying levels of market maturity requiring totally different approaches both in terms of marketing planning and the structure of the system.

It became critical to gain total acceptance of the importance of marketing issues throughout the corporation and in all disciplines to introduce common marketing processes in the company in such a way as not to stifle creativity, and to develop skills in all areas of the discipline appropriate to the various needs.

Achieving these goals, it was felt, would lead to the creation of a marketing ethos within the company from which a market-led operation would emerge.

The company needed 700 marketeers worldwide, and it was decided to look for them within the company and create them in the company's own image.

There are now clear definitions within ICL of the responsibilities and duties of individual roles within the marketing community.

It was found that the majority of people within the company were completely ignorant of what marketing was. Not only did they need to be shown how to do it as second nature, they needed to be shown what it was and why it was necessary.

They started with a series of courses based on mainstream advanced marketing theory plus best practice, using the marketing elements of the MBA, tailored to the information technology market and ICL's needs in particular. The programme took approximately fourteen days and was subdivided into five units: marketing strategy, explaining 'why marketing?'; segmentation and resource, based on a computer simulation of marketing activity, and addressing both the segmentation of markets and competitive dynamic; distribution and promotion; pricing, policy and strategy, and workshops that drew together all the lessons learnt in the previous events.

Some 800 people went through this training, and approximately 1800 attended a further three-day event for those members of the company who related closely to the marketing function.

The programme was attended by all those involved in marketing, ranging from graduate entrants through the main board directors. Now, everybody, no matter what their grade or experience, is required to go through it if they are to become involved full time in the marketing discipline. It has evolved from a purely training function to a worldwide support function.

Any company can move from being a product-led organization to one which is market led, provided there is top level support from the top executives, and some strong, some might say fanatical, champions of the cause. It will also help if there is some sort of external resource available to back up the champions' case. There then needs to be work related programmes and a general understanding throughout the company of the need for changes in the working environment, career levels and responsibilities, skills requirements, learning styles and reward mechanisms.

Changes on this scale require massive investments of money and time, and everyone needs to accept that it is a long-term process which will need continual, though varying, levels of support.

Not many companies are attacking the problem in as whole hearted a manner as ICL. Although all major UK firms pay lip service to marketing, most of them are still talking about sales and production, and they only humour their marketing people during the good times. When the bad times arrive they go back to staring at the bottom line and ignoring the long-term strategies.

In America it is different, the value of marketing is much more deeply understood by top management. In a recent survey of senior managers in America, Korn/Ferry International, the executive search consultants, discovered that 34 per cent of top executives came up through marketing, against 25 per cent from finance and accounting and 24 per cent from general management. The same survey predicted that this percentage would drop in the next ten years to 27 per cent, though not because of an increase in the finance or general management areas, but because professional and technical backgrounds will be providing 13 per cent of chief executives instead of today's 7 per cent. Marketing, it is predicted, will still be the largest supplier of top executives in the US.

In the UK we have not yet reached those giddy heights, with finance still providing the background for most chief executives, and hardly anyone making it from a professional or technical background. Where America leads in these matters, however, we generally follow, and it is a sensible trend for companies to adopt.

Too great a concentration on the financial aspects of a business is not always healthy. Unless you get the right products and create a need for them within a market that is able to afford to pay for them, there won't be any money for management to handle or plan for. Once a company is more concerned with handling its money than in marketing its services or products, it has already accepted, if unconsciously, that it has reached the top of its growth curve. It may still continue to be extremely successful at making profits, but it will cease to be an exciting company for anyone except the accountants to work in, and it begins to become vulnerable to attack.

By watching the bottom line too closely, and by building profits every year, a company may lose sight of the bigger picture. You may be able to hone your current operation to such a degree that it makes wonderful profits when these are compared with turnover. Overheads and wastage may be pared away to virtually nothing and the company may look like a star. But what if the overall market is expanding at an even faster rate? What if your actual market share is decreasing, despite the fact that you are running such a tight ship? You may have polished up your operation perfectly, but you are left with a perfectly polished peanut, a mouthwatering prospect for a larger and hungrier competitor to gobble up when it is looking to increase its market share still further.

Not many companies can afford to ignore the broader picture, and that means they need to practise the arts and crafts of marketing. As this realization becomes more widespread, and companies that are doing the right things are seen to be successful, marketing professionals will grow in corporate status. Once more marketing professionals reach the top of the corporate ladders, as is starting to happen now, so the emphasis will change and a snowballing effect will take place with marketing-driven companies increasingly forcing their competitors out of business.

The whole point of marketing people is that they can anticipate the needs of the future and frame probable satisfactions for those needs. What, you should be asking yourself, are the employment needs of future companies likely to be? How can you make sure you are making the right career choices in the first place?

It looks increasingly as if the free market economy is going to be growing and spreading for some time, even more so now that the eastern bloc is opening up to the concept of competition. Marketing skills, therefore, are likely to be the skills of the future.

At the same time the management experts are all predicting an end of the old-fashioned hierarchy of management, and an increasing prevalence of the 'flat organization'. Companies are, after all, nothing more than collections of individuals, and as individuals become more educated and skilled, and realize that they are able to exercise control over their own destinies, they are going to be less inclined to accept the sort of political nonsense that large companies traditionally inflicted on their employees. Marketing experts will be taking their skills to the organizations that appreciate them, and will not be content to be second-class citizens. It is already possible to see which those companies are likely to be.

If marketing people are trained to predict the future, they should also be able to see their own futures within industry, and at the moment all the signs are positive. No one has yet been able to discredit the basic concepts of marketing. These concepts seem, at the moment, to be the only way of ensuring the long-term success of an organization.

In order to create strong and successful companies from scratch, marketing must be the first consideration. Financial planning and control are just part of this process, ensuring a secure base and healthy growth rate. If a company looks at the finance first and then fits the marketing plans to the financial targets, it is less likely to succeed in the long term. All the most outstandingly successful companies in the world are marketing led, and the Japanese as a nation have proved over and over again just how far you can go with the right foresight, planning and product mixes.

Anyone who is looking for a career which is likely to take them to the top, and a profession which will give them the broadest base from which to work towards fulfilling their ambitions, is bound to consider marketing.

Building a career requires as much strategic thought at the beginning as building a business. If you are planning to build a company, you look at the whole market and analyse which sectors are growing and which are shrinking before making any decisions. It is the same with planning careers. It may be that the best career opportunities exist in the shrinking industries, simply because fewer bright people are going into them. Alternatively it may be obvious to the career planner that certain high-growth areas are going to provide the opportunities that will suit them.

The marketing world can provide niches for an enormous variety of different skills and should be considered by anyone intending to follow a traditional business career, either in the short or long term. Even if you are a potential entrepreneur, a well-planned marketing career will provide you with the most valuable experience from which to launch yourself into business. If you intend to end up as chairman of a multinational giant, the marketing department looks like the most promising place to start your climb.

Those who have chosen marketing as their profession are currently in the right place at the right time. The whole industry is gaining the sort of respect and credibility it deserves. Critics – those perhaps who believe success is all a matter of 'selling' and 'cashflow' – are gradually having to admit that companies that take marketing seriously become more successful than those that don't. As that realization spreads and the industry matures there will be greater opportunities for those who work within it; better training is already becoming available, and a variety of clearly mapped career paths are becoming visible through the mists.

It isn't only the marketing profession that is changing however, the whole business world is always in a state of evolution, but never before has the rate of change been as fast as it is today. Many of the experts expect that this will increase rather than decrease over the coming years.

To start with, barriers are falling all round the world, so that the globe is truly becoming one market for more and more product sectors. This is providing enormous opportunities for companies to sell their goods, but also enormous strains as they try to stretch themselves further and further.

At the same time, of course, more and more people are entering the market as producers as well as consumers, so competition is hotting up all the time. This trend is exacerbated by the recent trend for the lowering of barriers to enterprise through privatizing public companies, encouraging entrepreneurship, deregulating industries and developing international standards to allow business to move across borders.

At the same time technology is changing the way people work, with some able to work from home and others able to sell their specializations more easily to a number of different companies. Through developments in communications small companies are able to behave like large companies in many ways, increasing the competitive noise and sometimes stretching their own people to breaking point.

There are many other changes in the employment field; women and ethnic minorities are being brought into the managerial workplace in greater numbers, and companies are becoming less status conscious and more results orientated. Those who have a track record for solving problems are going to be able to sell their services to a variety of customers; those who rely on the fact that they have achieved a grand-sounding title in one company may find themselves in a less powerful position.

All this is leading to a speeding up and slimming down of the business world. With more companies competing for a place in the market there are more products being launched than ever before. You only have to look at the supermarket shelves and remember how they looked a few years ago to see how the trend is going. Yet at the same time, companies are looking for ways to cut their overheads by tightening up their teams and their operations. Many have done so using outside specialists rather than large in-house teams. This is a trend which is likely to continue.

The number of mergers and buyouts has also increased, causing further speeding and slimming, and often resulting in fewer people doing more work.

All these factors add to the picture of people being less able to rely on staying with a single company for the whole of their careers. As Rosabeth Moss Kanter says in her book *When Giants Learn to Dance*, 'If security no longer comes from being *employed*, then it must come from being *employable*.' Those who want to build careers must constantly be asking themselves if what they are doing today is adding to their saleability for the future. Will it look good on your CV?

Wise companies are also recognizing this trend and they realize that in order to attract the best people they have to offer them 'learning opportunities'. Recruits want to see that they are going to have the chance to improve their skills and make themselves more saleable in the marketplace. Paradoxically, the companies that are best at providing these opportunities for their people to move on, are also the ones with the best records for keeping people, because they are generally more enlightened employers in other respects as well.

Some people advise an even greater degree of cynicism on the part of employees. Paul Hirsch, in his book *Pack Your Own Parachute*, advises readers to:

remain emotionally separate, resist the temptation to get drawn into a corporate surrogate family, maintain visibility, marketability, generality, credibility, and mobility. Do this by cultivating networks, returning recruiters' calls, avoiding overspecialization and avoiding long-term and group assignments.

Overall, Hirsch advises people to think all the time of their CVs and ask themselves before starting every assignment whether the experience will make them more attractive to future employers. This is an extreme view of the way things will go, but it certainly has more than an element of truth in it for everyone who wants to ensure their own survival.

If we are moving away from the traditional career structures, where everyone worked their way steadily up the career ladders at a predetermined speed, we are looking at a very exciting future with a great deal of independence for those who wish to grasp it. There will, however, also be a corresponding loss of security which some may find hard unless they prepare for it.

3   *Should I have gone to university?*

Anyone who hasn't been to university is always bound to ask themselves whether they would have done better with a degree under their belt. Those who do get degrees might equally ask whether they would have gone further with three to five years more work experience instead.

There is an age-old snobbery about university, which suggests that anyone destined to be 'officer material', i.e. a manager, has to have a degree to start them off. Although that attitude, fostered to a large extent by organizations like the Civil Service, is finally becoming out of date, another more practical meritocracy is arising in its place.

Most people will accept the importance of training of all sorts and the need for highly-educated people to run our industrial and commercial worlds. The first step to becoming one of these people is generally seen as being the acquisition of a sound university education. The proportion of top managers in big companies who have degrees is unlikely to decrease, and it may even increase in the next few decades.

There are many successful people who are not university educated, but who have walked the 'university of life', and will swear that they have worked harder and done better as a result. Those people probably took the right decision in going straight into the job market, because it suited their temperaments and needs. If you are desperate to get out into the world and start work, so desperate that to spend another few years in an institution of learning will leave you bored and frustrated, then you had better follow your instincts. If you have sufficient ability then you will soon have gained enough experience to compete with contemporaries who have got degrees. By the time you get to the top of your profession – assuming you have the necessary innate skills for top management – people will be judging you on your practical track record, and whether or not you have been to university will be largely a matter for small-talk.

There are plenty of companies looking for bright young school leavers, particularly in the retailing sector, who will be happy to provide day release and other opportunities for further education. You may even be able to get the best of both worlds by gaining an Open University degree at the same time as work experience. Alternatively you might choose to follow a completely different course and spend five years doing something like an army training, which will give you a number of unique selling points when you enter the general job market, although it might mean you have to start at a lower point in the corporate structure than your university-educated peers.

No degree is an adequate replacement in the short term for on-the-job experience and a hands-on apprenticeship, but it is a valuable addition to it.

How much a degree helps in the long run is a constant source of fascination to careers analysts. The answer seems to be that if you add up your 'lifetime's earnings' to date, you will almost certainly have earned much more by the age of thirty if you have skipped university and gone straight into work. You will, after all, have been earning for all the time that the others were away studying, and your experience will be worth more to an employer than the services of a graduate with no prolonged work experience.

By the time you are forty, however, the graduate will be catching up, and possibly overtaking. The career opportunities open to graduates are, on the whole, more extensive than those on offer to a school leaver. An employer is able to make certain assumptions about a person who has a good degree and who has had a few more years in which to demonstrate personal abilities, even if those years have not been spent in a traditional job. When you take on a school leaver of seventeen or eighteen it is harder to judge their future potential than it is to judge a graduate of twenty-two. The school leaver who has been with an employer for five years, however, is of considerably greater short-term value to an employer than a fresh-faced graduate full of grand ideas on how to put the economy to rights but no experience in selling baked beans off the shelf or cars off the forecourt.

The training and work experience offered to graduates on arrival at their first jobs, however (albeit at lower salaries than the school leavers are earning by that time), will probably provide the basic equipment for much better jobs later on in the career pattern.

Everyone now agrees that a successful career needs to follow a continual learning curve, which is bound to involve formal training and retraining courses along the way. Some of these courses are open only to people who have degrees. It would be hard, for instance, to get anyone to take you on for an MBA course without a degree in your background to indicate you have the academic abilities to cope with the course. If you have achieved a degree in business studies, you will be able to short-cut your way through things like the MBA, since you will have done much of the preliminary work already.

At the beginning of a career everyone needs to know what you are capable of, and it is almost impossible to prove how useful you are going to be to a company when you haven't done anything before. The very fact that you have undertaken a university course and succeeded in getting a degree provides the prospective employer with at least one signpost as to your potential.

Marketing is a highly competitive industry, and is likely to become more so. There are many people out there who are going to be just as good at the work as you. Whenever you are up for a new job or a promotion you are going to be up against other people, some of whom will have degrees. Given that all other things are equal, an employer is likely to choose a person with a degree over someone without one – it is simply one more 'reason to purchase' – and if you are planning to get to the top you need to amass as many of those reasons as possible.

Unless you have a very clear career plan in your mind and you are confident that spending time at university will hinder rather than help that plan, then it would always be advisable in the long term to get a degree.

Those who are already out in the marketplace, and have made their way up the ladder without the help of a degree, however, will find that there are a growing number of professional qualifications offered by bodies such as the Chartered Institute of Marketing, which will add the necessary formality to their CVs.

Does it matter what sort of degree I have?

In the US there is already a wide variety of business degrees, many of these majoring in marketing. This is beginning to happen in the UK, and is likely to become more common. At the moment, however, there are very few people in the jobs marketplace with degrees which are strictly relevant to their current jobs, or to any jobs they are likely to hold in the future.

In an ideal world we would all know exactly what we wanted to do with the rest of our lives by the time we were eighteen, and would be able to plan accordingly. Again, in America, a surprising number of young people do know exactly what they want to do with their lives, and choose courses and holiday jobs to fit their career patterns. That is not the case in Britain. Most people are still 'busking it' until they are well into their twenties, perhaps only falling into marketing by accident, and then discovering that they have actually chosen the right path for themselves.

Given that there are still very few strictly relevant degrees available, it really doesn't matter what your subject is, as long as you can prove that you have a lively and disciplined mind and an ability to solve problems. The issue is as much about the quality of the degree as about which subject it is in.

Most high-fliers will have a second-class honours degree, first grade, but it is important not to concentrate all your energies on to the academic side of university life. Employers want to hire well-rounded, balanced people who are going to stay with them and be able to cope socially as well as intellectually. They are not looking to fill their companies with brilliant boffins who never want to come out of their back-rooms. Take time to join societies and indulge in outside activities such as sports – anything that will give you something to talk about at interviews and indicate that you have a spark. You need to demonstrate that you are able to achieve things and get on with people in a variety of situations.

If you are fortunate enough to know that you are going to be pursuing a career in marketing from the start, perhaps because your parents or other relations are in the business, or you have had some work experience, or you know a great deal about the industry for some other reason, then the more relevant the degree the better your chances when pitching for jobs against other graduates.

Again, if all other things are equal, an employer is likely to look more favourably on someone who has a degree in business studies and marketing than someone who has one in classics, particularly if the owner of the business degree has a clear idea of where they want to go in their career.

Given the way that the world is going, a course that has mixed marketing business studies with languages would be perfect, but whether you could find such an animal when you need it is impossible to predict.

All through your career it will be true to say that you can't have too much education or too much training. It can be obtained at any time, but it is cheaper and easier to obtain at the traditional ages. If you take off two or three years in your late twenties or early thirties to take a degree you are going to be sacrificing a lot of salary and missing out on an unknown number of possible career breaks, whereas at nineteen or twenty you are probably still finding your way and will not have a high earning potential in the marketplace.

If your eventual goal is to cross over into general management, a business studies degree is going to be very helpful in speeding up the process. It will mean that you have received a basic grounding in many of the other skills you will need to add on to your specialist marketing skills.

To those who are already out there working, experience is generally more important than a degree, but you may find that you lose out to competitors who have been to university when all your other qualities are evenly matched. As a result you may have to work harder, or gain other unique selling points for yourself, in order to compete successfully.

For those who are still trying to decide whether or not to take a degree, the answer must be that if you are in any doubt, then you should do it. If you know that you want to get into marketing then try to find a course that is relevant. If you are still unsure what path you want to take through life, just choose a subject at which you feel you will be able to excel and that you will enjoy.

Once you have embarked on a university course, see it through to the end. Nothing will put potential employers off more than seeing that you didn't stick at something you started. The ability to set yourself a goal and then achieve it is probably the most important signpost you can erect to guide other people towards recognizing your abilities.

4   *Know yourself*

The most important ingredient for success in any walk of life is self-knowledge. Unless you know who you are and what your strengths and weaknesses are, you will never be able to build a successful career. It is all part of the maturing process, part of which, of course, consists of learning by your mistakes. This is hard to do at the beginning, and the ideal situation is to become sufficiently self-aware at an early age to start making the right decisions as soon as possible.

Imagine that you are setting out on a voyage. You need to know who you are, where you are going and what you are going to be taking with you before you start. You will then need to work out how you are going to get to your destination.

You must decide what you are good at, and then find out where your talents are best fitted to take you. To get to your destination you will need some portable skills that will be gained through training and work experience. The means of getting to your destination will be the jobs you take on and the methods of approach you adopt with prospective employers.

A successful career happens when you correctly match your skills, achievements, experience, strengths and potential to the needs of your employers. To do that you need to ask yourself, 'what do I have to offer a prospective buyer of my services?'

Ask yourself honestly what your skills are. Are you good at handling people, or skilful with data? Do you prefer working on your own or in a group? What have been your outstanding successes and failures so far? What would your ideal job look like? Are you equipped to get a job like that or do you need to go through some more preliminary stages? Where would you like to live and work? How much money do you need in order to live happily? What are your strengths and weaknesses? What sort of person are you? What are your underlying values? – because it is no good working for a company if you disapprove of what they do.

You will not be able to build a full picture overnight; in fact you may never get a full picture, it is like a jig-saw to which you will find new pieces as you go along. Sometimes you will take on tasks you never dreamed you would be suited to, and will excel; at other times you will be offered exactly the sorts of opportunity you always felt you needed, and will prove unable to exploit them satisfactorily. The more knowledge you have at the beginning of your voyage, however, the more likely that you will make good decisions.

Self-deception is the worst danger for anyone hoping to build a successful career. It is no good setting up a radar system to check that you are on the right course if you then edit the signals to reflect what you want to hear rather than what is really happening. Lester Korn of Korn/Ferry puts it succinctly:

Know yourself. Know what you can do well, (and presumably what you can't do), and what will make you happy. Merge the two into a goal, then set off in pursuit of it.

The 'happiness' part of the equation may sound rather trite, but it is important. If you enter a profession with qualms about whether you are actually going to enjoy practising it, the chances of success are very slim. Anyone who is working because they have to, not because they want to, is almost invariably going to stay at the bottom of the ladder.

When employers are considering who to take on for a job, they are looking for certain qualities. If you are to 'sell yourself' successfully you need to know whether or not you have those qualities. You can't expect the interviewers to notice things about you that you haven't noticed yourself. Do you, to start with, have the right personal traits? Anyone going into marketing needs to be able to exhibit an air of confidence and a high level of inter-personal skills from the start. They need to be gregarious, self-confident and assertive. They need to be able to demonstrate clarity of thought and a determination to get into marketing. They need to be able to 'sell themselves' and possess a willingness to go out and find what they want from life.

Some of these attributes we are born with, some are developed by the home and educational environments in which we are brought up, and some don't come until later in life. In the end, communications skills are more important for a successful career in marketing than educational qualifications. These skills are usually natural, but they can always be honed and developed. If, however, they are completely absent, it would be better to recognize the fact and find a career option that will better suit your character.

You will, of course, change and develop as you go through life, and so you must be constantly amending your picture of yourself, checking that your goals are still the same as they were when you last chose a job to go after. You will have changed through increased experience, new achievements and greater insight into what you are capable of and good at. Only by keeping an eye on how the product is developing will you be able to tell when it is time for changes in direction.

University might be the first place where someone starts to come out of their shell and blossom, or this might happen as a result of travel or gregarious hobbies and social lives. It could be triggered by anything, from outward bound courses to the reading of novels, it all depends on the make-up of the individual.

In the majority of cases people do not discover all these truths about themselves until they are in their first jobs, and they then have to do some radical rethinking about whether they are setting out on the right paths at all.

It helps, however, to be aware of the need for self-knowledge early on in your career, and to set out in search of it as soon as possible. Marketing is generally an extrovert business, and anyone who is not comfortable in that sort of atmosphere will not thrive. It would be better to find this out at the beginning, rather than embark on a career that is bound to lead to frustration and failure. Equally, you might be too extrovert for marketing and be happier in the sales field, dealing with more tangible results, managing more people and being more directly involved in the front end of the business.

It is possible, with some help from experts, to ascertain more or less scientifically which sectors are likely to be suitable for your personality, and which are going to be totally unsuitable. Any process that even marginally cuts down the options at the beginning of a career is going to be useful.

There are consultancies that specialize in providing psychometric tests and career interest inventories which will show where your talents and interests lie. (Psychometrics is the measurement of psychological variables such as intelligence and aptitudes. It is the mathematical design of psychology tests and measures.) The tests could be undergone at any stage in your career, but are often used by young people trying to see where they should be heading, and by older people who feel they may have taken a wrong turn, or who merely feel that they have become stale and need a change.

To some cynics the tests are about as reliable as horoscopes or palm reading, but many believe that there is a lot to be learnt from them, and at least they start people thinking about themselves and about the ways they should be going.

What generally happens is that the clients (for a fee of around £200), will sit a half-day of written and visual tests under exam conditions. The results of the tests are then analysed and presented. The client is invited back a few weeks later to discuss them with a consultant on a one-to-one basis. Even if you don't believe that the tests have provided an accurate picture of your personality and aptitudes (though the majority of people seem to feel that they are accurate), merely talking things through with someone who understands the careers marketplace and has experience in counselling people could help to clarify your thoughts and expectations.

With personality tests the idea is to assess factors such as leadership skills, independence, capacity to serve others or to exercise authority, and the ability to meet the challenge of competition. If the demands of a job are in accordance with your individual personality you are much more likely to be happy and successful.

Saville and Holdsworth are career and vocational guidance experts, publishers of psychometric tests and providers of consultancy services for companies with roles they want to fill. Their job is to assess the skills of individual managers and provide the necessary skill-training career courses.

When a client company decides it wants a new marketing director, for instance, Saville and Holdsworth will look at the skills and abilities needed. The chances are that they will be looking for a mix of competencies, including both marketing and general management skills, depending on the level of the job.

At the top level of management they are looking for strategic and planning skills, an ability to create strategies rather than implement them. Senior people need to be able to develop good relationships with other departments, which will require high levels of inter-personal skills. They need a sound general business sense and social confidence. They need a gestalt of skills such as an ability to look at abstract problems, an interest in using data to guide their decisions, a willingness to look ahead and to plan well in advance. They need to be able to see the distant horizon while passing the minutiae of problems on to others so that they don't get bogged down. They need to be motivated into stretching the organization as well as themselves, and to create a feeling of success within the company.

Tests can measure all these things and can indicate whether individuals are able to prioritize and make decisions, whether they are able to see the business as a whole and to communicate effectively both orally and in writing.

On the purely marketing side, candidates for jobs need to demonstrate an interest in analysing people, in getting to know their clients and in climbing inside their heads. Only if they are willing to do this will they be able to make constructive marketing decisions. Depending on what sort of relationship they will have to the marketing campaigns, they might also need an aesthetic interest in the visual impact of things.

Companies are often looking for people who are willing to be experimental, to look at new ways and approaches to old problems. They need people who can create enthusiasm and hype around their products and services, which requires an optimistic, positive outlook and an ability to inspire the team with the same feelings.

Good marketing people will need to be able to communicate emotional energy and must be competitive. They must have a strong desire to get ahead of the competition, which will go with an interest in analysing their campaigns and products. They need to have a hunger to win, which will mean constantly analysing the enemy.

They also need to have creative ideas themselves, especially if they are going to be in the thick of the campaigns rather than simply managing the efforts of others. If they are managers of professionals then they need to be able to create a climate in which the team can be creative.

By doing a number of different tests, a company like Saville and Holdsworth can measure candidates' performances against a number of different criteria, using several sources of information, making the rating more objective.

There are occupational tests, which are multiple-choice tests of abilities and skills in the verbal, numerical, diagrammatic, mechanical, spatial, clerical and dexterity fields. They are psychological tests used in the world of work. They aim to maximize objectivity by standardizing test conditions, instructions, time, content, scoring and interpretation.

Then there are occupational interest inventories, which provide a structured analysis of a candidate's relevant interests, based on self-report. They contain a wide sample of questions which might cover hobbies, school work or general life experiences, which seek to measure the direction in which an individual wants to go occupationally. Interest inventories are particularly widely used in career counselling, but can also be used in selection, backed up with a selection interview.

Management exercises are simulations of management behaviour which can be observed and assessed in a structured manner. Occupational personality questionnaires give a profile of the candidate's perception of their relevant behaviour, and work profiling systems are techniques for analysing jobs and specifying human resource requirements.

The foundation stone of any assessment procedure is a full understanding of the job or career path in question. Companies like Saville and Holdsworth have computerized selection systems which manage the collection, analysis and storage of information gathered about candidates. In large-scale recruitment exercises they are able to rationalize considerably the work of interpreting and integrating data, especially at remote sites. A computer system can collect and store candidate data, carry out application form sifts, provide non-technical interpretive reports, analyse strengths and weaknesses, automatically produce all communications with the candidates, and establish a database for later monitoring and evaluation.

Few orgazizations have the necessary resources to construct their own tests, but some may commission the writing of new tests or parallel versions.

Some ability tests, known as attainment tests, are designed to assess the results of formal education and training – while aptitude tests measure the ability to acquire further knowledge or skills. Attainment and aptitude tests are in fact very difficult to distinguish in terms of content alone because measures of aptitude always rest to some extent on prior knowledge. For example numerical aptitude tests usually assume that candidates understand the basics of the numbers system. Aptitude tests do try, however, to avoid very specialist knowledge which few candidates would have the opportunity to acquire.

If you do nothing else, however, you need to sit down and think carefully about what you want to achieve and what your capabilities are. You need to be able to form a strategic sense about yourself, to see where you are going, or at least to see what options are open to you. You will then have a better idea of what information you need to find in order to make the right decisions about what to do next.

Dave Francis of Richmond Consultants, argues in his book *Managing Your Own Career*, that there are seven main 'talent clusters': self-expression, caring/helping, working with things, applied science, administration/management, physical prowess and influence/persuasion.

People with high self-expression have artistic, creative and expressive talents. They exploit inner intellectual, emotional and physical resources in ways which others appreciate. Those who have this talent will feel that they have something important to say and contribute to others. They will be effective in the marketing arena because they will have ideas and they will be able to explain them to others convincingly.

Those whose talents lie in the caring/helping area are committed to improving the quality of other people's lives. If they can find the right niche within marketing, i.e. working with products which they truly believe to be life-enhancing in some way, they will be dedicated workers and will consequently have a high chance of success.

A talent for working with things will lead people to the manufacturing and technical industries. They prefer to have definite tasks to perform. The growth of computing in all walks of life has led to an increased demand for these talents in white-collar jobs, which goes some way to compensating for the drop in opportunities within manufacturing due to the automation of so many processes.

Talents for applied science will lead people towards supplying specialized services, associated with complex information handling and decision-making processes. These people like methodologies and using valid, repeatable experiments. In the marketing field they are particularly suited to research and testing jobs.

A talent for administration/management comes from being able to organize and coordinate resources to achieve specific objectives. People with these talents are able to set goals, communicate their intentions, plan and coordinate. They are ideally suited for marketing, particularly if they see it as a path to general management.

These days physical prowess is not needed for most jobs, and a talent therefore usually finds its outlet outside work on the sports field.

A talent for influence/persuasion is possibly the most important for anyone entering the marketing and management fields. Anyone who can get others to do as they suggest, to buy their products and services, will succeed. A talent to influence is a talent to lead.

Everyone has a mixture of talents and it is a valuable exercise to work out where you feel your greatest strengths lie.

5   *What else have you done?*

As we said earlier, the Catch 22 situation for anyone embarking on a management career is that people need to know what you are capable of doing before they are willing to risk giving you a job. Until you have the job, however, it is hard to show what you are capable of.

One way of demonstrating your abilities is by gaining a good degree, and a business studies graduate who has done a business placement year may even be marketable enough to side-step a graduate training programme in one of the major companies and go straight into a marketing assistant's job.

Gaining a degree, however, is by no means all you can do to impress people. Prospective employers are looking for evidence of imagination and initiative, determination and perseverence, and all the other qualities that go to make up great managers. You could demonstrate that you have these attributes in a number of different ways.

Rather than staying at home between leaving school and going to university you could go travelling, picking up jobs as you go, broadening your horizons, meeting people, gaining self-confidence, and enjoying yourself at the same time.

Try to put yourself in the shoes of the prospective employer who is confronted by a number of seemingly identical would-be marketing executives, none of whom have any formal work experience, all of whom appear to have the same qualifications. One of these applicants has spent his summer in South America working with a voluntary organization to save the Amazonian rain forests, while another went on a package holiday to Ibiza. The former had no contacts to help him, he merely got himself down there on a cargo ship and went knocking on doors until someone gave him a job. The other one persuaded his parents to lend him the money for the holiday, and plans to repay them from his first salary cheque.

It immediately becomes obvious which candidate is the one most likely to succeed, and although this is an exaggerated example, it illustrates the case. If you make yourself interesting you will be noticed; if you show that you are not afraid to go out there and have a go, you will win the respect of the person who is interviewing you. Apart from anything else, however, you will have increased your own inter-personal skills.

It is often a wise decision to take a year 'out' between school and university anyway. It is much more likely that you will make a wise choice of degree course if you have had some time to reflect on what you want from life and what you are good at.

Work experience

If you are fortunate enough to know right from the beginning that you want to get into marketing, then you can utilize any spare time between school and university, or during vacations, to gain experience on the ground floor of your chosen profession. If you select a number of companies that you think could be the sort of firm you would like eventually to work for, find out the names of the marketing directors and write to ask them if you could join them for work experience, you will almost certainly find someone willing to take you on, and pay you the going rate for the job.

There is little chance that the job they give you will be interesting – they know after all that you are only going to be there for a few months – but you will have gained experience of what it is like to work in a large company (most of the companies able to offer this sort of opportunity are likely to be large). This will give you a huge advantage over someone who has done nothing, and who still has a number of misconceptions about how things are going to be.

It may be that having sampled the horrors of commuting or the intricacies of office politics you will decide that this sort of life simply isn't for you. Alternatively you may come across some specialization while you are working that you had no idea existed, but that interests you, and that you decide to pursue. Whatever happens you will have something to talk about at later interviews for full-time jobs, and your prospective employers will be able to make some accurate judgements as to whether or not you have understood the things that are going on around you.

If you are lucky enough to be taken on for work experience by a company with which you would actually like to start your full-time career, you have already climbed up several rungs of the ladder before the dice have even been thrown. A company that has accepted you for work experience and likes you will probably be very open to any suggestion that you should join them permanently at a later date. Knowing that you are interested in a long-term career with them will also make them willing, even keen, to offer you more interesting jobs and training opportunities while you are there temporarily.

Since few of us, however, are lucky enough to know exactly what we want to do at this early stage, most people will just get whatever jobs they can. The trick is to try to find something that will be different and interesting, and that is not too easy. There are some tremendous opportunities for people who really want to get going in life, but they have to be sought out.

It would be more impressive to tell a prospective employer that you ran a seaside fish and chip stall, and managed to double the owner's profits for the season, than that you went to the local factory and got a job as a sweeper-up. Any work experience is better than nothing, but anyone who is going to achieve a lot in the marketing world should be able to show that they can have fun and make decisions at the same time.

The armed forces provide examples of the scope of opportunities available for young people who choose to seek them out – particularly those who decide not to go to university. Someone in their early twenties could be driving tanks, flying fighter aircraft or navigating giant ships around the world while their peer group in the business world are still doing their best to understand why their cars keep breaking down on the M1. Such an individual could be applying for jobs in industry having become an officer and completed a first career, while university graduates are still having to compete for the same jobs with no actual proof of their potential.

Obviously there are political considerations to be taken into account, and not everyone would want to subject themselves to the rigours of service life even for a limited period, but the armed forces do demonstrate just how much responsibility it is possible to take on at an early stage if you so choose, and if you can convince someone of your ability to handle the job.

Extra-curricular activities at university can also say a lot about a job applicant. Companies don't only want to hire people who are able to achieve academic distinction. Often it is more impressive that someone has achieved recognition on the sporting fields or through running societies and clubs, provided that they have been able to maintain a reasonable academic level at the same time.

The secret is to decide what you would find interesting to do, and then set yourself a project with a definite goal that you can point to later as an objective achieved.

Using extra-curricular activities to boost your career does not end with the achievement of getting your first job. All through your working life people are going to be looking for evidence that you are a well-rounded personality, an achiever and someone who succeeds at whatever they attempt. Employers who are impressed by people who have no interests outside their work are not the best people to work for. They are demonstrating a short-sightedness which does not bode well for the future of their companies, or for the futures of anyone working for them. Employers need to encourage their employees to lead active and happy outside lives, whether that means running marathons, organizing charities or renovating the family home.

6   *Growing a tree*

Peter Needham, of career consultants Gardiner-Hill Needham, likens the building of a career to the growing of a tree.

By the time you get to the top branches, he explains, you are being buffeted by some pretty strong winds. If the trunk of the tree is flimsy, or the roots do not go down far enough, a strong wind will snap it in half, or drag it up out of the ground. In order to ensure that you can cope with life at the top, you need to put down deep, firm roots, and grow a thick, sturdy trunk at the beginning of your career.

In the same way you could liken the process to building a house with firm foundations and well-designed and strongly built walls. The principles are the same and the message which Needham says has to be got across to people at the beginning of their careers is: 'don't panic – you are going to succeed!'

The danger with bright and ambitious young people is that they will become impatient and try to move too fast too soon. They will be tempted to join companies that offer them short-cuts up the ladder; they will try to avoid spending years learning their trade and will attempt to go straight into high-flying managerial positions.

Ambitious young people are frequently arrogant and easily flattered by someone offering them a quick path to success. The terrible, boring truth is that there is no such thing as a quick path. Everyone who succeeds in any profession does so on the back of the experience they are able to pick up on the way.

It is better to take a job that pays less but teaches you more about the fundamentals of your profession, than to be making more money or taking on grander titles than others of your age. The fast track is very seductive, but anyone who allows themselves to be persuaded to get on it before they have learnt how to drive is destined to crash in the long term.

One of the most valuable first steps is to get out into the marketplace and find out how it works, which in most cases means selling. Although selling experience is not essential for a career in marketing, it is extremely useful. It demonstrates a willingness to tackle hard jobs and to learn. It also helps someone to develop the right personality traits for selling themselves at a later date.

Selling as a profession is becoming increasingly important as buying operations become centralized. The supermarketing scene is the best example of this, where a handful of giant names controls the whole market, and sales people who interface with these customers are dealing with contracts that can make or break their employers.

There are other skills to be attained at this stage of your career, and it is not necessary to worry about whether or not you are moving upwards yet. By moving horizontally in integrated skills you will be creating a broader and firmer base of experience upon which to build. You will also be able to sample a number of specialist areas, any one of which might catch your imagination and prove to have the potential for building a career.

All through someone's career there are certain factors that are going to be overriding simply because of the age you have reached. While no one should feel restrained to behave like everyone else in their age group, there is little point in trying to tackle certain problems when you are at completely the wrong stage of your career.

Up to sixteen years of age you are just concerned about what school to go to in order to get the best possible education. From then until twenty, your main concerns will probably be what qualifications to go for.

Up to twenty-three your main problems are deciding what sort of organization to join, and finding out what is available in the marketplace. Until you are thirty you can be deciding how far you intend to go with your career. Your self-confidence will grow during this period and you are looking for breadth of experience and depth of training.

Between the ages of thirty and forty most people are spending a lot of their energies on bringing up children and their main worry is how to keep going at work and fulfil commitments to the family. This is a highly demanding time, when people who are going to be high-flyers will start to achieve really big things, while trying to keep their marriages and emotional ties intact.

Around the age of forty to forty-five you are half way through your working life and you may start to ask yourself if you are going to keep on doing the same things for the second half. This is sometimes known as the 'mid-life crisis'. Some careers have obviously reached plateaux at this stage, which may mean you want to move on to greater things elsewhere or devote more attention to your personal life. You need to be very clear about what your aims and priorities are at this stage.

For the next twenty years you will probably have reached a relatively calm period, where you have accepted your limitations or are enjoying the fruits of your success. You will be able to become statesman-like and help others up the ladder behind you. You will have more time to reflect and think strategically, rather than rushing around getting things done on a day-to-day basis.

From fifty-five or sixty onwards, careerists have to ask if they are ready to stop work. If not, they have to look for ways to adapt to different opportunities. There is now plenty of time for thought and assessment.

While it is always good to have a long-term view of where you are going, there is no advantage to impatience. You need the strength of getting it right at the early stages in order to achieve the greatest rewards at the end.

7   Choosing an industry sector

For many people the industry sector in which they take their first job will be the one they stay in for the rest of their careers. It is possible to swap sectors later, or to move into a related business, but on the whole people stay put. The experts suggest that you should, at the latest, know in what industry you plan to build your main career by the time you are thirty.

This is therefore one of the most important decisions that anyone makes in their life. Yet for many of us the decision is almost arbitrary. We are offered a job by someone and it fits in with our immediate plans, in that it pays the right money and is based in the right geographical area, so we accept, and we have set the pattern for the rest of our lives.

If we chose our spouses in such a haphazard manner it would be surprising if we ended up with happy marriages. Of course many people will make mistakes in both areas, and these can be rectified, but in changing horses mid-race we slow ourselves down and cause upheavals and unhappinesses that might have been avoidable with a little research.

If graduates were to put half as much work into researching the sector in which they want to work as they put into researching their university theses, or if school leavers prepared for their job interviews like they prepared for their exams, they would stand a much better chance of getting it right first time. Someone who manages to back the right horses from the start of their career is going to be doing much better in the long run than someone who has one or two unhappy years before working out that they are in the wrong place and then trying to do something about it.

It is relatively simple to research the world of work. There are the newspapers, which are full these days of information on industry and commerce, plus innumerable books and magazines available in public libraries. For school leavers there are careers offices and for those who have been to university there is even more information made available. Nearly all sizeable companies will be happy to talk to graduates, either on the milkrounds or individually, and will supply them with relevant background information.

Most people entering the job market have only the most hazy of ideas about how the world works, when a little research would explain everything.

A good graduate will receive any number of job offers from companies making the milkrounds of the universities, and often the decision about who to join is made on the strength of the company, which is fine, but with no regard to the industry in which that company operates.

School leavers may not receive quite so many tempting offers, but then there is not quite the same urgency to get into the right place immediately. Any good company is going to provide them with the work experience they need to be able to compete in the job market later on. That doesn't mean, however, that a high calibre applicant should take the first job offered; they should make sure they go to as many different types of company as possible in order to get as clear an idea as possible of what they have to offer.

There is a world of difference, for instance, between the fast moving consumer goods markets and the information technology industry. One is a mature marketplace with a well-accepted structure and fairly predictable growth patterns, while the other is an emerging industry which still has a massive growth potential. The first is full of very mature and very skilful marketing companies, while the latter has a few giants and hundreds of hopeful young companies jostling for space underneath. A mature industry can often be the best training ground for somebody setting out, since the companies are experienced and know exactly what they are doing, whereas a young industry offers the possibility of a more entrepreneurial approach to life.

There are declining industries, and industries that have already declined and are now ready to be picked up and shaken back into life. There are industries that are labour intensive and likely to be put out of business by competitors in the Far East and other areas rich in cheap labour. Some industries involve selling millions of products a year (like baked beans), while others involve selling one or two (like the aerospace industry).

There are many clichés and preconceived ideas around about all these sectors, some of which are accurate and many of which are ludicrously out of date. Only by actually going to see for themselves can potential recruits find out what it is like on the factory floors and in the offices.

Straight into consultancy

Some of the brightest university graduates might be offered places in the high-flying world of management consultancy, with famous names like McKinsey and Bain. School leavers, or those who have not gained very good degrees, will probably have to wait until they have industry experience before they can hope to be taken on by these companies, though their positions may be all the stronger as a result of the wait.

The offers made to high-flying graduates, however, are likely to be very tempting. New recruits would immediately find themselves mixing with senior management in client companies, involved in serious strategic decisions and moving quickly from one project to another. Although they would not be able to run projects themselves at the beginning, having no experience that can be sold to the client, they would be very close to the centre of the action. The money would also be higher than that offered anywhere else.

For those who know what they are doing, and are happy with the possibility of being trapped in the world of consultancy for longer than they might wish, that is fine. But this is the fast track, and it is a dangerous path for anyone looking to get to the very top of the business world.

Recruits who spend the first five years of their careers as high-flying consultants are going to become accustomed to the excitement and to the money. The successful ones may become urbane, smooth and clever operators, but if they then decide, as many do, to get out of the consultancy world and to ease up on the pressures of continual travel, they might find it is harder than they thought.

During their years as consultants they have probably never been involved in the implementation stage of their suggestions for a client company. They have never actually had to take the consequences of their own actions, as someone involved in the launch of a new fmcg brand or the development of a new car would have to take the consequences. Their track record as consultants may be faultless, and they may be able to pick and choose jobs in the consultancy world, but they may find themselves limited to that world, and they may find that it begins to feel restricting and unsatisfying.

There is a right time to go into consultancy, which we will talk about later, but for anyone hoping to get to the top in marketing, it would be better to resist the lure of the fast buck and fast lifestyle until you have the experience to back it up.

The important thing is to choose a sector which is established enough to offer the right amount of training and career back-up, but still on an upward growth curve. Above all, however, it must be a sector which the recruit finds exciting and which they could imagine staying with for the whole of their working lives if nothing else materialized – even if in the end they find that they are moved on to other things.

Beware of fashion

It is always tempting to move into sectors which seem to be talked about as being 'hot'. At one time it was the computing business, then it was financial services and anything to do with communications.

While all these sectors offer some very genuine career opportunities, perhaps to get in on the ground floor and grow with the companies concerned, they are nearly always new industries with little or no structure in their approaches to marketing or to the training of marketing people.

An industry that is booming too ferociously is almost bound to suffer a number of set-backs before settling down and maturing. If you are sure that it is a sector that will hold your interest until the end, none of these factors will matter, but if you have merely chosen it because everyone has told you it is a growth industry, you might find in the long run that it is less fulfilling than a more traditional and established sector.

Fashionable sectors on the whole are good places for people who have gained experience in the more established sectors to exploit their knowledge; they are not often good places for beginners.

In the computing sector, for instance, it soon became obvious who the giants were as the industry settled down, and these companies now offer career development potential every bit as structured and thorough as the fmcg companies. In the financial services sector some of the big insurance companies and building societies are beginning to show themselves as the front runners in the marketing race, although anyone who has served a full marketing apprenticeship in an fmcg company might be surprised by just how amateurish some other sectors still are in their approaches to marketing.

8   *Choosing a company*

Choosing a company for which you would like to work is never an easy decision, but it is hardest at the beginning of your career when you have little experience with which to compare the packages on offer.

Yet the decision is vital. If you get it wrong it will not be the end of the world – you can always make a change later – but if you get it right you may have set the pattern for the rest of your life. There are still companies which offer such good internal career development opportunities that all their senior executives have come up through the ranks. This doesn't mean to say that you should expect to stay with a company all your working life, but if you get the first choice right you may, with a bit of luck, be on your way to a long and happy relationship.

You can't have too much information about a company before you join it. This is almost as serious a step as marriage – in fact over the years you may be spending more of your waking hours with your work colleagues than with the spouse of your choice. You need to go into the relationship with your eyes wide open, and you need to know exactly what is going to be on offer.

It is not easy to find out about the world of work while you are on the outside, but it is not impossible. To start with you need to analyse what contacts and sources of information you already have available to you. Do your friends or family work for companies which are of interest to you? If not, do they know of anyone who does? Any contact like this could lead to an appointment to chat to someone about the opportunities and to make your desire to work for the organization known. There will also be information available on most major employers at careers offices and at some local libraries and job centres.

If you have the courage, you could phone other sources of information within the company's market sector, such as their professional institute or the editor of a trade paper; or you could phone a careers office or a national newspaper to ask if they have any information in their offices that you could look at; or you could ask whether they could point you towards someone who does have such information. The chances are that a professional institute or newspaper will keep extensive libraries of background material on companies and careers, (the Chartered Institute of Marketing is a prime example of this, with a library which contains more than enough material to satisfy the curiosity of any job seeker).

You should ask the help of anyone you know who is already in the world of work, from parents to teachers, next-door neighbours to family friends. Apart from anything else, all this research is a perfect grounding for someone planning to work in marketing. It is the first stage in the marketing plan for yourself. You are finding out what it is that the customers (employers) want and need, so that you can set about providing it for them.

If you are still hitting brick walls you can approach the personnel departments of the companies you are interested in with a direct request for information, which in most cases they will be happy to send, and you can then go back to them with a request for an appointment to go in to talk to them. There doesn't have to be a definite job on offer at this stage, you merely want to get a feel of the company and to let them know that you are interested. If you approach them with a well-written letter, explaining why you would like to know more, they are going to be willing to see you. If you turn up at the appointment on time, decently dressed and groomed and showing that you have already done some background work into them, they will be impressed.

When you get to the interview be sure that you have a lot of questions to ask, but be sure also that the questions are founded on some research of your own, so that you can show you have read up on the subject, that you are serious and that you are not wasting their time with frivolous enquiries. By asking about training opportunities and chances of promotion, you are demonstrating that you have a long-term intention of staying with whoever you join, and of developing a career with them, rather than just taking the first job offered out of expediency. When you are there, ask if it would be possible to talk to other people who have recently joined the company, so that you will get an idea of the sorts of experience you can expect. They may say no, but this in itself will tell you about the sort of company it is and about the degrees of openness they adopt.

The more research you do at this stage the more accurate a picture you will have of what it is going to be like working for a particular company, and the less likely it is that you will be disappointed by a job which is nowhere close to your expectations when you turn up for work on the first day.

The package the company uses to tempt you will consist of financial incentives including salary and perks, training schemes and a company culture. The last two elements far outweigh the first one. If you get your career development right, the money and perks will always follow; if you chase the money alone it will almost certainly elude you, as will the more important reward of job satisfaction. Provided you are getting enough money to meet your immediate needs, you can concentrate on the opportunities and training the company is offering, and on the culture. Ask yourself: why am I taking on this job? What will it lead to within the next two years? Is it going to fit into a longer-term game plan?

Company culture is something few people think to investigate when they are about to start new jobs, yet it is probably the most important element in the mix. All companies have a culture of some sort. They have certain codes of conduct and appearance which may not be written down anywhere, but which are generally accepted and are probably set by the top management. Just by looking around at the way everyone behaves an outsider will form a good idea of what is expected of people.

If everyone in the boardroom is ex-military and sports mad, the chances are that these values will permeate down the ranks. There will be a general atmosphere of discipline mixed with male camaraderie and competitiveness. There will probably be a lot of neat haircuts and well-pressed suits. If you are a woman, or a man who is more interested in reading and visiting the theatre than getting your hair cut and joining in with company football matches, the chances are that you will find it hard to get on in the company and that you should look for an environment more suited to your tastes.

In other more entrepreneurial companies people may come to work informally dressed, and spend a lot of time talking business in a social atmosphere. If you are uncomfortable without a structured working style where you know what your job is and how you are expected to carry it out, you might be uncomfortable in this sort of environment.

Because good people are hard to find, a company may well offer you a job even though you aren't set in their usual mould. No doubt you will be able to handle the job they are giving you very adequately, but you have to ask yourself whether you will actually move up the company very fast if you are not in tune with those around you.

It might be tempting to think that you will manage to fit in and adapt either yourself or them, but in reality people like working with others who are like them; as a result successful companies retain their character with only minor adjustments down the years, and anyone who is not comfortable there will have a harder time getting to the top.

In many cases it will become obvious very quickly that you are in the wrong place. Many would-be marketeers start off by believing that they would like to work for companies like Procter and Gamble. When confronted with a job application form which asks questions like, 'What do you want to have achieved in ten years' time?', the majority give up half-way through. Most people at twenty have no idea of the answer to that question, and the very successful companies can afford to wait for those who do.

Try to spend as much time as possible inside a company before you agree to join, and meet as many of the line managers stretching up above you, to see if they are the sort of people you would want to mix with and emulate. When you go for an interview make it known that you would like to see round the company and meet people. If you don't ask, they will probably not offer and you will leave the premises having met only one or two of the people in the personnel department and having seen the reception area and the personnel manager's office. If you ask for a guided tour and a chance to talk, and if they are interested in you as a potential employee, they will be happy to arrange it in order to show you the places where you would actually be working and the people you would be working alongside.

As you talk to people and look around their places of work, ask yourself if you are comfortable with their views on life, or whether they would start to irk you after a few months or even years in the company. Is it, for instance, expected of employees to work late every night and take work home at the weekends? Or do they prefer a more relaxed approach? Does everything that happens have to be ratified by a dozen meetings and twice as many memos, or are managers left to their own devices and allowed to make decisions and then act on them without too much interference from above?

Do the canteens and recreation areas give the impression that the company cares about its people and wants to keep them happy, or do they just seem to be doing the minimum to stop people leaving?

It could come down to the most mundane physical details which seem trivial but which over the years would add up to a bad match. One company, for instance, might keep a luxurious head office in the best area of London or some other sophisticated metropolis, while another might prefer to operate from offices over their factory in some desolate part of the country which happens to suit their distribution network. If you are a Persian carpet and Picasso in the boardroom type, you may not be happy in an environment of works canteens and well-worn office furniture. Different types of company appeal to different types of people, and you will not be happy working in an atmosphere that doesn't please you.

9   *Large or small?*

The biggest difference between companies is generally size. There are pros and cons to joining large or small organizations, which need to be weighed up very carefully, particularly at the beginning of a career.

The big companies provide you with a strong brand name with which to start off your CV. Most managers are more comfortable employing people who have worked for companies they have heard of. It is easier for them to be able to justify their decisions; 'I've just hired a bright young chap from Mars', is going to sound more impressive than, 'I've hired a bright young chap from some engineering company'. It goes back to a well-known saying that 'no one ever got fired for buying IBM'.

The blue chip companies are also the best equipped to offer you the sort of training you are likely to need to be successful in the future. Anyone who sees that you have been trained by a name like Procter and Gamble, Mars or Unilever will make certain assumptions about your abilities. The fact that such sought-after companies wanted to take you on speaks volumes for your abilities, and the fact that they are all well-known training grounds for future managers will also make you more attractive to future employers

Not everyone, however, is comfortable in the big company environment, even for a few years. They feel stifled and lost. It is much easier to shine brightly if you are one of a dozen trainee managers than if you are one of a hundred. Smaller and newer companies will be able to offer you more visibility and responsibility more quickly, and may provide a steeper learning curve.

If you have found a small company that you feel sure offers you exactly the package you want, and you are confident that you can see a future either with that company, or by using it as a stepping stone to something else, then that is the right decision to make.

The problem with starting with a small company, however, is that it is hard to move to a bigger organization later. You will almost certainly move up the ladder faster than your equivalent in one of the giant organizations, but should you decide that you want to move on to a bigger pond you will find that you may have to take a drop in status, if you can persuade them to take you on at all. A training with one of the big brand names will make you saleable to almost any other sector or style of company, but a training with an unknown, however good the training and however genuine your progress up the management ladder has been, will be harder to turn to your advantage.

On the other hand, a small company may spot your abilities and start to give you genuine responsibilities sooner than a large organization with a set way of doing things. There may be more flexibility and more opportunities to take responsibility in the small company. You will have to pay the price of a less thorough training and grounding in the general business world but possibly more real decision making and responsibility at an early stage.

As with the decision on whether or not to go to university, there is nothing to say that you won't be more successful by choosing a small company and growing with it than you would have been as one of a crowd at a brand name organization. If, however, you have not been able to find a company that you are confident will provide what you want, you should look at the biggest and most prestigious names first – there is always a reason why these companies are held in such high regard.

10   *Continuing your education*

The first part of anyone's career is basically a continuation of their education – in an ideal situation of course the whole of one's life should be a continuation of one's education – and we need to resist the temptation to 'start work' before we have to. A company that offers to train a new employee in the broader subjects, perhaps even agreeing to fund an Open University course, will be more useful in the long term than one that offers training in specific job skills.

The job skills are going to have to be learnt as you go along, of course, but a firm foundation for future managers needs to be as broad and deep as possible. General management training schemes that move people around from department to department are less common than they used to be, but companies that are utilizing their staff well still offer a variety of experiences in the first few years, without expecting to get back too much useful work in return. They are investing for the future, and you should be willing to take advantage of every skill and scrap of knowledge they are willing to give you at the beginning. It will all help to strengthen the trunk of your particular career tree. The opportunities to show what you are capable of achieving in the way of results will come along soon enough.

All through their careers people who want to succeed are going to have to be searching out the best training opportunities. In some companies the path is well mapped out and the individual simply has to follow the plan laid down. In others the senior managers might not always see the benefit of training in certain skills and subjects, and the individual will have to convince them of the need.

The career drives

In order for training to be successful, participants have to be able to see the reason for it. They have to be able to see what's in it for them if they are going to get anything from it. If they feel that they are being 'sent', rather than choosing to go of their own free will, all the trainer's efforts will be wasted and the trainee will gain nothing from the experience. Different people want different things from life and from their careers, and will therefore have to be motivated in different ways to take training courses.

In his book *Managing Your Own Career*, Dave Francis of Richmond Consultants, a management development and career development consultancy, claims that there are nine major career drives: material rewards, power/influence, search for meaning, expertise, creativity, affiliation, autonomy, security and status.

'Material rewards' covers all the tangible assets which contribute to our standard of living and provide us with wealth which, in turn, gives us power and status. Some people would see this as their prime motivator, and if they treat it as such will probably be successful at attaining their goal, provided they are able people. They may, however, gain wealth at the expense of other satisfactions. It is a cliché that 'money doesn't bring happiness', but like most clichés it is often proved to be true. As part of a mix of drives, however, a need for material rewards is normal and healthy enough. People who are motivated by material things may resent taking the time away from their desks to train, unless they can be persuaded that they will be able to increase their earning power as a result.

Seeking to have power and influence over other people and over resources is another element that works well as part of a person's make-up, but can lead to personality problems if it is not balanced by other factors. Someone who always wants to dominate others may have trouble listening to advice, and they may be tempted to make decisions for short-term political advantage rather than long-term considerations. This driving force will, however, give people high levels of self-confidence and clear ideas about the right way to do things. Training gives these people another tool with which to pursue their goals, although they may be disruptive influences in the classroom, reluctant to submit to the authority of the trainer.

'Searching for meaning' sounds rather esoteric, but it is a key element of a balanced personality – someone who seeks out opportunities to do things that are valuable for their own sake. The criteria could be religious, emotional, moral, social or intellectual, but strong convictions will help someone to keep going in a chosen direction and will help them to avoid being distracted by superficial temptations along the way. It could be seen as the 'moral backbone' of someone's personality upon which other drives and abilities can be hung. These people contribute a lot to whatever causes they take up, including their careers and the other people involved with them. People with these drives will see training as a possible way of finding out more about themselves and about the world in which they are working. They will also question anything they are taught that they feel goes against their beliefs.

Expertise, meaning the seeking of a high level of accomplishment in a specialized field, gives people confidence and stimulates them to work long and hard in order to increase their competence in their chosen fields. If this is your primary drive you may be uncomfortable moving into general management, preferring to stay within your own specialist skill area. The general work environment is moving in favour of people taking this path. Many companies are coming to see the value of hiring independent experts in different disciplines rather than keeping large in-house staffs. They are also beginning to see the value of rewarding people highly for specializing, so that there is no status or material reason for having to strive to move into general management if that is not where they would be best suited. These people will always be keen to train at anything that builds on their chosen knowledge base.

Creativity is an important part of marketing, and someone who has original ideas and is able to turn them into reality is a valuable asset to any company. People with this drive enjoy breaking new ground and are generally philosophical about setbacks. These people may be impatient with training procedures unless they are seeking a specific skill which relates to their creative ambitions.

People who are driven by affiliation make good team members. They want to be close to others and enjoy human relationships. Sometimes they stay in unsatisfactory jobs just to be with people they like. They will be willing to undergo training in order to build up relationships and endorse team membership. They will be helpful course participants, acting as bonding agents and team builders.

Those driven by autonomy want to be independent and to make their own decisions. They do not react well to bureaucracy but make good leaders if they manage to get that far. They tend to make good entrepreneurs and self-made people, not liking to be restricted by others. They may react badly to training, not believing that it is relevant to them unless they can see a direct and immediate benefit.

Security is a common drive and is found within most people to varying degrees. If it is too dominant it can lead to a reluctance to take risks. These people look for predictability and are happiest in companies which offer stability and have a track record for looking after their employees. Security seekers are the ones who prefer to have other people look after their career structures, but paradoxically they are the ones who most need to take their fates in their own hands if they want to be sure of what is going to happen to them in the long term. They will be keen to undertake training that will increase their worth to their employer and thereby increase their security.

Those who are seeking status will be happy to undertake training if they feel it will enhance their position – perhaps with an MBA or something tangible and visible at the end. They are impressed by symbols and will undertake whatever courses are necessary to build their own prestige within their peer groups. They want to impress others and one way of doing that is through qualifications.

11   *Changing industries*

There could be a number of reasons why you decide to change industries. It might be that you made a mistake with your first choice, or you simply didn't know that an industry which has since caught your attention even existed. It might be that you decided to go into one sector because of the training opportunities on offer, but now want to put your skills into practice somewhere else. It might even be that you simply feel like a change.

There is a definite pecking order in the marketing world, with the fast-moving consumer goods companies at the top, followed by consumer durables, retailing, financial services, industrial, and public services, in that order. It is easy to move downwards and very hard to move up. If you have trained in one of the blue-chip fmcg companies you will have no trouble persuading somebody in one of the other sectors to employ you. If, on the other hand you have started in the industrial sector you stand next to no chance of persuading an fmcg firm to consider you half-way through your career.

That is not to say that you will actually be moving into an inferior job in any way by going from an fmcg company to an industrial company, it is simply that some industries have been practising marketing for longer and have a greater need for marketing skills. As a result they have become better at getting the best marketing people to join them, and at developing these people. Some industrial companies still don't have a marketing department (or they may have one in name but it would not be recognizable as such to a marketing person from the fmcg sector). They are not therefore able to offer any sort of structured training to a newcomer to the business, at least nothing that would later be of any use to an organization selling frozen foods or chocolate bars.

If you have trained in a company at the top of the marketing tree, however, you have skills that all the other companies are coming to realize they need. Marketing as a profession was virtually unheard of in Britain twenty years ago. It was introduced by the big multinational American companies who have since proved its value beyond a shadow of a doubt. Other industries, as they become modernized, either through choice or necessity, are bound to start looking at the things the most successful companies are doing right. One of those things is the successful practice of the skills of marketing.

A well-trained marketeer, therefore, is a very valuable commodity to a company that has suddenly realized that having a technical department and a sales team is not enough. Moving to a company where a whole new department needs to be set up and motivated could be a far more challenging opportunity for someone than staying within the safe confines of the organization which first took them on. Equally it might be a nightmare, and one to be avoided at all costs. It depends on what sort of challenges you enjoy.

Relatively new industries, such as financial services and information technology, are desperate to recruit good marketeers. Although some of the bigger companies are beginning to be able to train their own people, they can't yet hope to do as good a job as the fmcg companies. Someone, therefore, who has trained with a blue-chip food company will be able to go to a financial services company with a basket full of appropriate skills that can easily be adapted to the new industry.

The styles of marketing will be very different in certain sectors, and will not always suit people used to other things. In the industrial sector, for instance, the marketing function is much closer to the sales and commercial disciplines, but the same applications of foresight and common sense will be required which can be formalized into a marketing function.

Headhunters and recruitment firms often talk about other jobs to young marketing managers who have trained in the big-name companies. The successful young marketeers are flattered and intrigued. It might be that having been with their mother companies since they started work they are feeling itchy feet and want to test out what their market value is. When they find out the sort of titles and rewards packages they might be able to achieve by moving sectors they become even more interested and go out to see what the companies are like. More often than not, however, they take one look at the outside world and dash back inside to their employers. One recruitment consultant described this as being like watching tortoises pushing their heads out to look around and then ducking back inside their shells, as if joined to them by elastic, when they realize just how well off they are.

It is not completely impossible, however, to move up the pecking order if you do it quickly enough. If you are young and bright and working successfully in a consumer durables company you might be able to move up to an fmcg company if you are willing to take a drop in salary and status. If you are used to earning £14,000 and having a car you might have to drop to £12,000 and lose the car. You might also have to drop to being a marketing assistant when you had already reached the grade of marketing manager. A willingness to make these sacrifices, however, will demonstrate your determination to succeed.

Most people prefer to move down the pecking order as they accrue experience, and up the status and salary ladders. For many, of course, the fmcg area holds no interest at all. There are different attractions in all areas of industry and commerce. The services industry, for instance, can offer everything from airlines to hotel keeping and catering, management consultancy and hairdressing, while at the heavy end of manufacturing there are mighty power stations to be marketed around the world as well as chemicals, pharmaceutials and engines for aeroplanes. In each of these sectors there are large and small companies, forward-thinking ones and ones that need to be pulled into the late twentieth century. Only by reading and researching about them and then going round to see them all and getting a feel, can a prospective employee discover which sector is the most suitable. With luck you will get the choice of industry right first time.

12 *To move or not to move*

Whether or not to move companies is often the most difficult decision anyone has to make. Even these days people still feel a certain loyalty, if not to their bosses then to their colleagues, and there is sometimes a feeling of guilt at taking training from one company and then, to all intents and purposes, selling it to another.

At the same time there is a fear that if you stay in one place for too long you are not fulfilling your full potential, that you are missing opportunities that may never present themselves again.

On top of this there is the conflict between staying with what is familiar and comfortable, and going out to conquer pastures new, meeting exciting new challenges and stretching yourself.

There is no one ideal path to follow. It will depend how good the company is that you join in the first place. If it is a very large, growing organization, capable of offering you rewarding jobs and challenges at every level of your career, then there is no reason not to stay.

It is worth remembering that 80 per cent of all job promotions are made from within companies. The odds, therefore, are that those who stay put move faster.

A shrewd employer will make sure that good people are given opportunities to move internally as soon as they begin to get itchy feet. If, however, you have become blocked and dissatisfied where you are, and don't seem to be able to change the situation, you would be ill-advised to waste two or three years wrestling with your conscience and probably doing a bad job at the same time, before deciding to move on.

There are extremes at both ends of the scales which will work for some people and destroy others, so let's look at the alternatives.

Staying put

If you are good at developing your career inside your company this could be the best possible way to get to the top. It is sometimes hard for senior management to be brought into big companies like Shell or BP at high levels, because they are not used to the corporate culture. If all the other senior managers have been working together for twenty or thirty years it is hard for a newcomer to break in. The management team probably has a language all of its own that you will never learn in time; you will always be an outsider. That may not be a bad thing for the company, but it makes it harder to land the top jobs. In some cases, such as post-privatization in companies like British Gas and British Telecom, new senior management was brought in specifically to change the 'way things were done'. If a senior executive is strong enough he or she will be able to move into any company that feels it needs that individual's particular skills. If a company does not need to make radical changes to its culture, however, it will more often than not need senior managers who have long experience of working within the structure.

This doesn't mean that you can't move into any large company halfway up the ladder and still be able to absorb the culture in time to get to the top, but it does mean that those with talent who stay the course from beginning to end may have an advantage in the climb to the top which is hard for newcomers to overcome.

If your company has been clever at moving you around and offering you new challenges, you will have been able to build up a far broader base of experience than would have been possible by chopping and changing companies. A large employer will probably move its promising people every year or two. Within a few years your CV will demonstrate that you have had a 'diverse background'. Had you done the same number of different jobs in different companies, your CV would have begun to make you look unstable and unreliable.

Supposing, however, that you have joined one of these giant companies at the beginning of your career. You might be one of two or three thousand employees who could possibly have the ability to become chief executive in twenty or thirty years time. There is going to be some natural wastage along the way, but basically there is going to be a log-jam of talented executives sooner or later – there simply are not enough top jobs to accommodate all the bright young people who are given management training courses. That is why these companies end up supplying talent to the rest of the business world. If some of the managers didn't leave, the companies would soon be top heavy, and unable to move up anyone from below.

You may be perfectly capable of ending up as managing or marketing director of the company, but so are a thousand other people. So are you willing to take the risk of being the one in a thousand who is going to make it right to the top, or would you rather take the experience and training that you have been able to achieve so far, and move somewhere where the odds on reaching the top are better – perhaps one in a hundred or even one in ten?

There are going to be stages in your career with any employer when you are going to see that the odds are against you getting much further up the ladder. You are going to have to face the fact that there are others around you who are more likely to get ahead. You then have to decide whether you are happy to stay where you are. It may be that you have reached a level which is perfectly acceptable to you. You may be quite happy to keep doing the same job until you retire, knowing that this is the limit of your capabilities. If so, then you should probably stay where you are and not move beyond your own abilities.

If, on the other hand, you feel that you could go further up the tree, and that you do have more to offer a company than your current employer needs from you, then you should start looking for new opportunities.

The longer you stay with a major company, however, the harder you will find it to move later on. You will increasingly become a corporate citizen, like the tortoises the consultant described. If all your friends work with you, and you are used to doing things in a certain way, it is going to be very hard to leave a company where you have a proven track record and start again somewhere else, having to prove yourself all over again to new bosses, new colleagues and new subordinates.

It may be that this is exactly the sort of challenge you need to get you started agan; it might also be the one thing that will upset your carefully balanced life and give you a nasty attack of ulcers.

Zig-zagging to the top

Let's look at another scenario. You have joined the company that promised you the best possible training, but now the training period is finished. After two years of being constantly moved around from department to department, perhaps even from country to country, learning exciting new things, going on courses and being involved in a mass of new experiences, you are suddenly given a rather mundane, less task-orientated and serious job to do.

The reality of the situation is crushing. You are bored and disappointed. You want to get back to the front line, and so you begin to look around for another company to join. You find one and you move. The new company is just launching a new product, so your adrenalin is racing again and you become excited and absorbed. Two years later, however, the product is launched and the work becomes a matter of daily routine – just keeping the stocks on the shelves and ticking over. Once again you become bored and fidgety. Without waiting to see if the product will become a long-term success you start looking around for another challenge.

Now, because you have been trained by a good company, and have been involved in the thick of a big product launch, you are probably very saleable, and you may find that other companies are still very interested in you. Do this two or three more times, however, and your curriculum vitae will begin to tell people another story.

People who zig-zag around too often do not get to see projects through from start to finish. If you are destined for the world of consultancy this may not matter, but if you are looking to become marketing or managing director of a major company, people are going to want to see a track record of perseverance, loyalty and solid achievement. No one expects you to stay with the same company from cradle to grave any more, or even to limit yourself to two companies, but if you can show that you have done a number of jobs thoroughly for three or four major employers in your career, you will become a highly sought-after executive. There are certain times when it is good to move, if that is what you want to do, but it is always worth exploring the possibilities of staying on first.

One major move by the time you are thirty would probably be ideal, and a good history with three companies by the time you reach the end of your thirties would also be encouraging to future employers. Someone who has moved about a few times in the past is more likely to avoid making mistakes in the future.

Look inside for opportunities first

Korn/Ferry International have done substantial amounts of research into the career patterns of the most successful corporate executives around the world, and generally speaking it is the people who stay put who get the furthest.

It also turns out that they are the ones who earn the most money. If you leave your current employer to take a job at 20 per cent more money, the chances are that your new employer will not give you a raise for at least two years. Had you stayed put, you would probably have had two or three raises during that time, taking you above the level you are earning in the new job. Almost everyone who stays put in their companies earns more in the long run, as long as they are not being blocked from moving upwards for any reason.

So when the urge to move strikes, it is always a good idea to analyse what it is that is wrong with your current employer, and try to put that right, before giving up and going off to somewhere where you believe the grass is going to be greener.

Good employers always want to keep good employees. If they do not go to any trouble to make you want to stay, then the chances are that you don't have much of a future in the company and should be looking around for alternatives anyway. If you are frustrated by the job you are doing or have a personality clash with your boss, a good employer would rather know about it and try to put it right than lose you without knowing why.

If you are able to get everything you want from the company you are with, and there seems no reason why they should not be able to offer you a structured career right up to the top of your abilities, then there is no reason to leave.

If, on the other hand, you can see that you are becoming stuck or are in danger of being shunted to one side and forgotten, and you can't get your company to do anything about it, then there is no reason why you should stay either. It may even be possible to leave a company and return to it later, having broadened your experience with another employer and made yourself more able to compete for jobs that were previously passing you by.

Every time you are tempted to move companies try to imagine what your CV is going to look like in twenty years' time. Would you be able to justify to someone considering you for a top job why you stayed in this company for only two years and that one for only three?

You are, in the end, going to have to show a track record of achievement, one that will make prospective employers believe that you are going to be of value to them – not that you are going to come in for a year or two and leave as soon as the novelty value has worn off. They want to hire people who are prepared to stay with jobs through the bad times as well as the good, and who are able to overcome obstacles in their careers rather than always walking round them.

Whatever happens you must be decisive in your actions. Many people who manage to be extremely decisive executives when it comes to making decisions about the direction their companies or products should take, are hopeless procrastinators when it comes to deciding what they themselves should do.

Any dissatisfactions and frustrations should be voiced and not held in and allowed to fester. Your employers can do nothing to improve your situation if they don't even know that there is a problem. They would rather you went to them and said, 'this is what I want to do with my career; I would like to do it in this company, but if I can't I will be looking for opportunities elsewhere next year'. They will admire your clear sense of vision and direction and, if they believe in your abilities to achieve what you want to achieve, will be keen to find ways of making you want to stay with them.

13   *Get a profit centre*

Before too long in the course of a career, you need to be able to prove that you can run a profit centre. When the chips are down any prospective boss, or existing boss considering you for a new job, wants to know if you are capable of delivering profits to the bottom line and of taking decisions that have direct impact on profits. Everyone wants to hire people who have problem-solving capabilities. To prove that you are one of those people you have to make sure you are in positions where the problems finish up.

Most managers do not have the opportunity to do this in their normal job. If you are concerned with market research, packaging, advertising, public relations or promotions, you are concerned with spending money, not with making it. You may be able to argue coherently for an increase in budget, you may be able to cut costs when required, or do any number of other brilliant managerial things, but you have never actually been answerable at the end of the day for the way the overall figures look, and that is the one thing that potential senior managers have to be prepared and able to do.

It may be that in order to get this experience you have to take a sideways or even a seemingly downward step. Do not be deterred! Explain to your bosses why it is you want to do it, in case they think you have gone mad, and so that they will be able to plan better what to do with you later when you have proved yourself up to the task. Insist that if you are not given the chance by them, then you will start looking around for a company that is prepared to let you have a go.

One way to prove your abilities in this area is through brand management. It is unlikely that the most successful and glamorous brands are going to be up for grabs, so you may have to agree to take on dull or ageing products which are in need of drastic surgery. This is a perfect opportunity to demonstrate what you are capable of. Anyone can make a success of a new and exciting brand with a mega advertising budget. (Obviously there are some notable exceptions, with brands that burst out on to the world and spontaneously fail. If you are carrying the can for one of those you will be able to prove your mettle through your abilities at crisis management.) However, few people can turn round a brand that is beginning to fall out of fashion. Someone who succeeds in a task like this will earn the undying gratitude of the company.

Equally you should seek out difficult, even crisis situations, because that way you will be able to prove what you can achieve in adversity as well as when everything is going smoothly.

If you are in retailing you might be given a run-down branch to revitalize; in the car trade you might be given an outlet that is consistently showing lower profits than average, and a brief to build it in any way you can. You might be asked to set up a new market for the company in a foreign country which has previously not been considered worth trying.

Your achievements might not make a big difference when compared with the overall turnover and profits of the group, but the managers who put you there will know what you were up against and will be able to judge the degrees of skill and flair you showed in handling the situation.

Were you bold and imaginative in the ways you went out looking for new business, or were you incisive in the ways that you cut overheads and rationalized the backlog of stock? Do you approach your business in a bullish or a bearish frame of mind? Were you able to motivate your people to perform better, or did you end up doing all the work yourself?

All these questions will provide an insight for the company into the way you might operate if you were promoted into general management and senior marketing jobs. It doesn't matter how humble the task you are assigned, it is the way you tackle it that will count for or against you in the records.

Alternatively you might ask to move across into sales management for a while. Although everyone at the serious end of marketing is quick to point out that selling is not the same as marketing, selling is the major part of the equation which makes up marketing, and anyone who has proved that they can run a sales force and can produce the right results, is going to be in a strong position to move up the corporate ladder when opportunities arise. You will also have gained an important insight into what impact the marketing decisions taken at higher levels have on the sales people who are actually out talking to clients and asking for orders.

The important thing is to stay with the job until the results come through. Anyone can rush in to revitalize a brand, come up with lots of wonderful new ideas for promotions and advertisements, cut overheads dramatically, and then go on to another job, leaving somebody else to carry the can for the demise of a product to which the death blow rather than the kiss of life has been administered.

In preparing for top management and putting down the necessary roots to support the branches of your career tree, you need to know, for your own confidence as well as the confidence of those around you, that you are capable of running a business. The earlier you can prove this the better.

One of the reasons why good people sometimes leave large companies in favour of small ones is because they want a chance to exercise their entrepreneurial talents – or at least find out if they have any. It is often possible to do this within the confines of your own company. That way you do not have to undergo the upheavals of moving, and if you fail you can always go back to your old job, or something similar, suitably humbled and chastened by your experience. There you can lick your wounds and think again about where your real talents lie.

14 Ready for the first change of employer?

You may think you are ready for your first move a couple of years after you join your starting company. The chances are that this is not so, unless you have made a bad choice of employer or you have realized that you would be more suited to another sector. If this is the case then it would be as well to move as quickly as possible, before you lose too much time and can no longer get into a new company or industry as a trainee.

When graduates are first taken into a management training scheme in one of the major companies, there is often something of a university atmosphere. You will probably be left to yourself most of the time to get on with your projects. You will be responsible for your own activities and looked after by the company. No one will expect you to produce measurable results.

Once you have moved into a brand or product management role however, things will change. Suddenly you have a specific, identifiable job. You are less able effectively to manage your own time and you will find you are having to take on a number of dull, humdrum jobs all related to one project or product.

At the end of your training scheme you feel that you have been turned into a number cruncher, stuck in a cubby-hole doing boring jobs you believe are way below your capabilities. A lot of people begin to look around for something else at this stage.

Before making a radical move, however, it would be worth taking some advice. Now might be a good time to undergo some psychometric tests, just to ensure that you are making the right choice, and that you are not simply suffering from the 'grass is always greener' syndrome. It is easy to become disillusioned with the world of work at the beginning, deciding that it is not living up to your expectations, when the fault actually lies with your own attitude. Perhaps it is your private life that is unbalanced and unsatisfactory, and you are blaming your work. Perhaps it is just that you can't accept the boring bits of the job which are inevitable in any position. Perhaps you had unrealistic expectations of how far and how fast you would be able to move in the first two years. Now would be a good time to do some serious analysis to check that you are in the best possible place and getting the best possible experience. If you are unhappy about anything, fix it now before it leads to long-term demotivation.

If you are sure that you want to remain in the marketing profession, but you think you need a different employer, it might be worth talking to one of the major recruitment consultants in the area. They will, in the long run, have a vested interest in finding you new jobs, but the best ones will also advise you if they don't think now would be the best time to move. They will listen to you and counsel you on what your options are. If you insist that you want to look at what is on offer they will be happy to comply. They want you to continue coming back to them throughout your career, and they want to safeguard their reputation among employers. They do not want to become known for always sending along people for interviews who subsequently decide that they don't want to move from their current employers or, worse still, take the job and then move on again a year later. But when the time is right for you to make a move they may be able to help you.

Some of the smaller recruitment firms will have neither the time nor the ability to counsel you on long-term career strategies, they will simply want to get you into a new job so that they can get their commission. As long as you understand this, there would be no harm in going to see a few other possible employers, if only to compare what they are offering with what you have already got. This will help you to evaluate your position and see whether it is as bad as you think, or whether you are simply passing through a dull phase or turning up a blind alley within your company. There will have to be a very good, tangible reason for moving at this stage.

It is important to stop and take stock of your position every few years anyway, and two or three years into your first job would be a good place for the first pause and re-evaluation.

Ask yourself what you have received so far in the way of training and job experience. Do you feel that the company has had your best interests at heart and has been making sure you get the right breaks? If you are not sure then go to your boss and ask how you are doing. It is important that you know what they think of you. If the news is bad it is better that you find out now, so that you can do something about it. If the news is good and they know that you are not completely happy with the way things are going at the moment, then they will be able to talk it through with you and decide what changes to make.

15 Gaining different skills

If you feel that you need fresh challenges and stimulations, now would be a good time to start building up on some new skills that will be useful to you later on. However good your job is, it will never utilize all your potential skills, and it would be unwise to let the unused ones become rusty in case you need them to compete later on.

You could, if you so choose, remain a dedicated marketing person throughout your career. You may never deviate from working in this specialist field, but you are limiting yourself in two ways. Firstly you are limiting your own comprehension of the broader business picture, making it harder to understand other people's points of view and priorities, and secondly you are limiting your chances of moving up into senior general management at a later date.

Although the statistics suggest that more and more chief executives are coming up through the marketing departments, that doesn't mean they don't understand and have experience of other disciplines as well.

In order to run a successful company you need to be able to understand the finances and how they work. Marketing people can be good at financial planning within their own areas, budgeting how much can be spent and predicting returns on investments, but they do not have to consider the broader picture of capital invested in a business in the form of new equipment or recruitment, of cashflows and borrowings, wage bills and interest rates.

Human resources is another area it is critical for potential managing directors to understand. While they may know the problems of hiring good marketing staff and what cars to give them, they do not know the problems of finding good maintenance workers, accountants, lawyers or cleaners, or how to structure pensions or maternity benefits.

A successful senior manager needs to be well rounded in order to bring together all the disparate elements of a company and get them working in harmony. Managers from a marketing background will always be looking at things from the marketing point of view, which is right, but they must not be blinkered to other ideas and standpoints.

Make it known inside the company that you would like to be able to work in the finance, personnel or general management departments, if only for short periods. That way you will increase your own knowledge base, improve your connections within the company, and rekindle the excitement you enjoyed when originally faced with a completely new challenge.

It is possible that you will have to take a drop in your remuneration package in order to do this, so it is important to plan for it to happen while your overheads are still low. By the time you have a large mortgage you will feel less inclined to take a short-term cut in pay for a seemingly distant long-term goal.

Experience in selling

Any experience at the sharp end of selling will be helpful to a marketing manager. Someone who has decided that they want to make their career in marketing doesn't have to prove that they are good at selling, but they do need to prove that they know how it works.

Unless you actually get out on the road at some stage, meeting customers, dealing with distributors, organizing point-of-sale material and explaining to the outside world why the company is doing what it is doing, you are always in danger of ending up inhabiting an ivory tower.

It is very easy for a marketing director to sanction a multi-million pound advertising campaign or promotion, forgetting the effect that that will have on the workload of the sales force. A shortfall in production, for instance, may mean that a marketing director has to decide which customers get their deliveries on time and which ones do not. Only with an in-depth understanding of the company's customer relationships can anyone hope to make wise management decisions.

All good companies will make sure that their marketing people spend time on the road with sales people. Anyone who really wants to know what it is like to close a sale or calm down a customer who hasn't received a delivery when promised, will have to go out and do it themselves at some stage.

Any talented marketeer who starts in selling will be moved across to marketing before long. It may be, however, that you turn out to be more talented at selling than you thought, and will not want to move on.

Most of the companies who are well known for their marketing expertise will ensure that their marketing people move around the business on their way up, in order to ensure that the company enriches and strengthens its own human resources. Many more will pay lip service to this idea but will, in the end, find it is hard to move people just when they want to, and will consequently slip back into bad habits, leaving people in one place too long, if not chivvied by the individuals involved.

A sales person who gets into a company that has the wrong attitude will only have one way to rise, and that will be through sales management. A marketing person in the same company may also only see the future as a straight line up through to major account executive and national account executive. Good people are soon likely to feel blocked in this sort of company, boredom will set in and there will be wastage as they start to look around for new challenges and more broadening experiences.

It might be more beneficial, both to the individual and to the company, if someone who starts as a sales person then moves across to be an assistant branch manager, and then moves on to spend some time in training – thereby improving their presentation and inter-personal skills – before going back into sales management for a while and then back to product management. This individual is going to have a much deeper and richer knowledge of the company, the products and the market place, than someone who has come in at the bottom of one ladder and worked their way up it.

The company will gain by intertwining and involving all the different strands of the marketing effort. It increases everyone's flexibility and means that those who are involved in the training process are fresh from the front line, and are therefore completely up to date in their methods and information. There is always a danger that someone who has been in a training department for six or seven years is going to be out of touch with what is actually happening.

Such highly planned internal movement is an ideal situation, but the reality in most companies is that the various channels are so far apart that they can never interlock effectively.

This sort of development of human potential within companies becomes far more important as the shortage of skilled people increases. As the trend continues towards making managers into 'implementors' rather than 'instructors', it also becomes more important that they are capable of making things happen in a number of different areas. It is helpful, for instance, if the company's strategists are not separated off into little pockets of expertise, but have been implementors as well, otherwise a company is in danger of creating 'them and us' situations at a later date.

The key word is probably 'flexibility', but this doesn't mean that companies should move people around just for the sake of it. All moves must fit in with an individual's personal skills and plans and at each stage the successful company will be asking themselves, will this move make this person more useful to us?

The general management experience available through the sales department is often greater than the equivalent experience in marketing. A marketing director might have only fifteen or twenty people in the department, whereas a sales director might be in charge of a sales force of several hundred.

A good time to get that selling experience would be at this early stage of your career. You have already established that you are a marketing person, so there is no danger of you becoming diverted into a long-term career in sales unless you so choose. You have in your first two years of training gained a broad picture of the company and of management generally, so you will be able to see whatever you do in the selling department in a wider context. You also still have the necessary energy and enthusiasm to tackle selling, probably the most gruelling of jobs for anyone who is not a 'natural'.

16   *Time for an MBA*

While everyone knows that you should continue taking training courses throughout your career, it is always easier to do them at the beginning, when you have more time, more energy and fewer pressures on you. If you can get the bulk of your business education completed while you are still in your twenties, you will then be able to keep yourself up to date on new developments with short, sharp training courses later on. Someone who is in line for a top job in their late thirties or early forties may find it harder to take a year off work to do an MBA, because the job may have been filled by someone else while they were away, and they will also have lost touch with the company and its markets, unless of course they take a part-time course, which would be an enormous strain running alongside a high pressure job.

Someone in their twenties, however, is more likely to do it if they have sufficient motivation, and the demands of their jos should be significantly less, allowing them more time for their studies.

There are a number of reasons to take an MBA. To start with it will significantly enhance your CV, particularly if you can get somewhere interesting like Harvard or one of the big international business schools in France or Switzerland. It will give you one more advantage over the opposition who have not got MBAs when it comes to competing for a new job. This doesn't mean that anyone who doesn't take a course won't succeed, it just gives those who do one more career development tool.

If you are preparing yourself for general management, but have so far only acquired specific marketing skills at work, then an MBA will teach you some of the broader skills of running a business from a more general management standpoint. This can be enormously beneficial later on, and it will help to do the groundwork early in your career.

There are two ways to take an MBA, and two ways to pay for it. You could take a year off work and study full time, or you could do it in your own time or on day release from your company. You could pay for it yourself or you could persuade your employer to sponsor you for it.

The ideal situation, of course, is to have a year off and to have your employer pay for it – that way you are demonstrating to anyone who is reading your CV at a later date that not only are you bright enough to take the course, but that your boss at the time thinks enough of you to be willing to pay the fees for you and to keep on paying your salary.

If this doesn't happen – and it seldom does – and you still want to take the whole course at one go, you are going to have to find the fees yourself.

Not only are you going to have to find the money to pay whichever of the management colleges you choose, you are also going to have to find enough money to live on during that year, to compensate for the loss of your earnings.

The theory is that you will at the end of the course be able to get a job at twice the salary because of the qualification, and that you will soon recoup your losses and go on to profit dramatically. This does happen, but you have to be very self-confident at the beginning to be willing to risk so much for a possible future reward. Again it is easy to see that it might become progressively harder to do this later in your career, although many people who feel they have become stuck in dead-end careers in their thirties or forties do try to use an MBA course to jolt them back into the mainstream. Sometimes this works, but often there is a good reason why they have not been progressing as fast as they had expected, and nothing they can learn on an MBA course will compensate for whatever is lacking in their basic make-up.

If the prospects of taking a year out from work are too daunting, then you are going to have to find a way to take the course in your own time, or on day release. It is more likely that you will be able to negotiate some sort of financial assistance from your employers if you do it this way, since they could be persuaded to believe that they will benefit immediately from your increased skills. You will, after all, be coming back from the classroom refreshed and full of ideas, and able to apply these ideas to your job. The potential workload for anyone doing it this way is high, but the results can be very worthwhile.

For example, Cranfield School of Management runs both kinds of MBA course. Their full-time course runs for forty-five weeks broken up into four terms. This is more intensive than many of the other schools, who spread the course over two years. The first two terms at Cranfield are the core programme, providing the basic functional areas of finance, accounting, marketing, quantitative analysis, organizational behaviour, human resources management and information systems, while the second two are the elective programme.

There are exams at the end of the first and second terms and the students have to pass these before they can move on to Part Two. Ninety-five per cent pass. The remaining 5 per cent usually drop out because they are not able to cope with the course for a variety of reasons. The high pass rate is generally attributed to the selection procedures at the college which ensure that only people who are likely to be able to succeed are accepted.

In the second part of the course students learn to apply the skills they have learnt into specialist areas like strategic management accounting, looking at typical management decisions and organizational issues. So in the first term you would learn core marketing. In the second term you would take this a stage further, perhaps by looking at international marketing, the marketing of services, or high technology marketing, with all the related issues. Students can choose the subjects they would like to cover in the second part of the curriculum as long as they gain the right amount of credits during the course.

The part-time course at Cranfield is identical in all respects to the full-time one, except that it is spread over two years. Part One takes up the whole of the first year, with the second year becoming Part Two of the programme. The part-time course also includes four residential weeks in any one year, and the students are expected to attend on sixteen alternate Fridays and Saturdays, so the pressure is on family life as well as on work.

To get on a full-time MBA course at Cranfield you would probably need to have had five years' work experience, a degree of class 2. 1 or better, and a good score on the graduate management admissions test. Other business schools do not all demand the work experience before accepting you, including it in the course in some way instead. Because they take a number of different considerations into account, there will be some students at Cranfield who do not have degrees or who are older than the average. Cranfield generally looks for people with the ability to complete the course successfully, and it will judge those people in many different ways.

During the courses the students are formed into management teams, with as wide a set of skills as possible, with each of the study groups being given a supervisor. They spend as much time discussing what they are learning as they do actually sitting in the classrooms. In addition, students read and study alone, and use the computer facilities to play business games.

Since 80 per cent of any manager's time is spent communicating, a large part of the course is devoted to inter-personal skills, and there is also an outdoor programme for personal development.

During their electives, students at Cranfield will often become involved in overseas projects, raising the funds themselves and managing the trips.

Anyone thinking of taking an MBA would be well advised to shop around several of the schools to see the different options on offer, and to find one which will put the least stress on home and work situations. Two years is a long time to be under intense pressure, and any way that can be found to alleviate this may make the difference between eventual success or failure. Costs may also vary between schools, and may be a deciding factor for some students.

When employers agree to allow someone the time off to take an MBA course, they seldom expect to receive less than 100 per cent of that person's effort on the job. If the job is demanding for someone working at it full time, it is going to be even more demanding for someone simultaneously undergoing the pressures of a training course.

Having an MBA on your CV will demonstrate a level of initiative and determination, and taking a course may well hasten a career change for you. Most people who finish a course take on a new job or at least new responsibilities very quickly.

The very highest of fliers probably will not want to stop and take the time off for a course, and will probably also believe that it is unnecessary for them. If they are true high-flyers such an assumption would be right, if they aren't quite as bright as they think they are, they may be missing an opportunity to climb an extra few rungs on the ladder.

It would, however, be a mistake to believe that an MBA is a panacea for a career or a life which seems to have come aground. The courses make good people better, but they do not change mediocre people into high performers. An MBA is one more career tool, but it is not a miracle worker.

17   *Forget about career development*

Although the main point of this book is to draw people's attention to the need to put some thought into planning and developing their careers, there will be times when you should forget about the future and just get on with the job, concentrating on giving a higher degree of added value to your employer.

Anyone who becomes too obsessed with thinking about where they are going and how they can use what happens today to further their own interests for tomorrow, is going to expend all their energies on being manipulative and scheming, and won't have time to get the necessary results along the way.

The secret of career development is to make periodic assessments of where you are going and how well you are doing; the danger is to become obsessed by ambition. In order to be successful you need to be single minded, but there are many dangers in becoming 'tunnel visioned'.

The most foolproof way to reach the top and be successful is to be good at your job and to have a record of success. If, after one of your periodic reassessments you have decided that for the moment you are in the right place doing the right job, you can then forget about planning for a few years and get down to learning the job and obtaining some results which will look good on your CV.

When the time comes for people to assess your track record in the future they are going to be more impressed by someone who has kept their head down and achieved a high level of success at whatever they are doing than by someone who is constantly popping their head up to look around and see if they are missing any opportunities by being in the wrong place.

Rather than judging yourself by how far up the ladder you are getting, or by what title and rewards package you are being given, it would be better to measure your performance on whether you are achieving the results in the job which are expected of you. Is your brand being as successful as it should be? Are you managing to revitalize an ageing product range, or are you managing to introduce an up-to-date marketing system into the company where none existed before?

Make sure that the results you are achieving are measurable and quantifiable in some way. Even if you are not in charge of a profit centre, there are going to be ways of ensuring that you are doing a good job. There are going to be figures to prove that you are achieving the results you were briefed to achieve, or that you are falling behind.

The best way to get to the top is to demonstrate that you can do the job. The best way to demonstrate this is to show that you have done it before, which means doing the job right today.

All the time you are working you are building your personal competence, hopefully with the aim of moving on to the next position that you desire. If you are known to be good at the jobs you undertake people are likely to offer you opportunities that will be denied to others. You need to be able to perform reliably to an acceptable standard in everything you tackle. Each time you move to a new job there are going to be new competencies which need to be mastered. It will always help in the transition if you have prepared in advance for the new challenges.

In other parts of the book we talk about the importance of continuing to learn and develop throughout your life. Changes are inevitable. Even if you don't want to progress in your career beyond a certain point, there are still going to be changes and developments in the world around you which will force you to move on, and not least of these is your own ageing process.

Anyone who wants to rise to the top should be asking themselves continually, how can I gain new competencies? How can I become more able? If you are continually improving the product which is you, and making it more attractive to employers, you will not need to worry about seeking out opportunities, they will start seeking you out.

It is a good idea to look for role models, people above and around you who you believe do a good job, and analyse what competencies they have that you don't have. Then you can set about gaining the same competencies for yourself.

18 *Continuous development and ongoing training*

British business is notoriously bad at training. The statistics vary depending on who you are talking to, but it is generally accepted that where some countries average several weeks of training each year for managers, Britain averages several days.

There are of course organizations that do it superbly, and they are generally the ones that do everything superbly. They are the famous names, the companies that know how to market, how to recruit, how to manage and develop their human resources. They are the companies of excellence every ambitious young marketing person tries to get into at the beginning of their career. Anyone who is established with one of these employers will probably not have to worry about the training aspects, it will all be laid out before them.

The sort of people who are recruited into these companies of excellence, however, are generally the sort of self-starters who are constantly aware of the need to gain new skills and brush up existing ones. Often they will be going to their bosses and asking for extra training before it is even suggested. These are people who are determined to succeed.

While companies can be berated for not offering their employees as much training as they need in order to excel, it is largely up to the employees themselves to ensure that they get it. Not only do most employees never think to go to their bosses to ask for more training, many actually try to get out of it when it is offered.

It is always easy to find excuses for not going on a course. To start with, good courses always cost a lot of money. They also take up time, the commodity most highly prized by most managers. Disgruntled customers and subordinates may be heard complaining that you are 'on another *** course' when they fail to get hold of you. There is a general suspicion that going on courses is an excuse for having a pleasant break from the routine of work in a country hotel somewhere.

In fact many training courses are extremely enjoyable, and anyone who goes on them generally comes back refreshed and revitalized, but that does not mean they are not a constructive way to be investing your corporate time and money. As long as you and your colleagues are continually learning and developing, none of the excuses holds water. Any training course that is well run and used at the right time will pay massive dividends to both the participants and employers.

The complaint many people have with training courses is the frustration the individual often feels when returning to the company and being given no scope to practise what has been learnt.

Many companies and individuals tend to think that training is a luxury which can only be indulged in once they have made some profits and have some money to spend. In fact it should be the other way round, with a training budget built in to ensure that the profit targets are met and surpassed. There will always be other more tempting things to spend the profits on when they finally arrive.

Anyone who is working in a company that does not have a sophisticated and well-planned training scheme for all levels of management, must make a point of finding out what courses are available in the marketplace and then lobbying the right people with the right arguments. There must always be logical reasons for any training. It always needs to be relevant to the needs of the company and the individuals; if it isn't part of a strategic plan, or answering an immediate need, it will be wasted. No matter how good the trainers are, training will only stay with people and affect the way they behave if it is relevant and applicable to their immediate needs and situations.

There is no point, therefore, in going too fast and taking courses designed for people with far more practical experience or different market needs.

There are basically four stages of a career into which training can be fitted. It starts with fundamental training for people who know nothing about marketing. This could mean someone who has been working as a sales person or a general manager in a small organization, and who has been asked to set up a marketing department for the company. It is also for the graduate or school leaver in their first job, and for general managers from other disciplines, to help them understand why marketing is important and what it can do for a company if handled properly and professionally.

The next category is 'implementation and practice', for existing practitioners who need to increase their general marketing skills within specialist industry sectors, or to increase specialist skills such as direct mail, public relations, sales promotion, market research, merchandising, pricing, product development, exhibitions or distribution, or related subjects like marketing law or finance.

Ideally these courses should be taken as the individual reaches each stage of their career. In reality they are taken when someone is suddenly given a new responsibility and they realize they know nothing about it, or when something has gone wrong in a particular area and they don't know how to fix it.

Changing industries or sectors can be another reason for taking some training. If you are a marketing manager in a major fmcg company, and you land the job of marketing director for a retailing or service company, you are going to need to adjust everything you have learnt, in order to aim at different targets. It will help to have someone with experience guiding you in the fundamentals of your new chosen industry.

Then come the advanced courses for people who are already well versed in the general skills of marketing, but who want to keep up to date on new developments and new techniques. At this stage you will also need to improve your personal skills and learn how to maximize the performance of your subordinates.

Finally you have the strategic courses, aimed at directors and senior managers who are directly involved with company-wide strategic marketing, including planning and implementation. By the time you have reached this level you will be responsible for planning the training of others and you will have to put into practice all the theories you developed along the way on why you as an individual would have been performing better if your bosses had only been willing to invest in more training for you.

How much time is spent on the courses will always vary. It is unusual for anyone in a demanding job to be able to spend more than a week away from their desk, although some of the management colleges do have courses which run into several weeks. For senior managers, even the thought of spending a week away from work can be daunting, and it is often better for them to take one-day 'overview' courses, which will provide a taste of what can be gained from longer sessions. During a day, delegates will be able to judge whether they know enough to make a longer course unnecessary, or whether it is an area in which they have dangerously large gaps in their knowledge, in which case they will be more willing to invest time in filling them.

For companies of any size it is usually more cost effective to hold training sessions in-house than to go outside. The disadvantage of in-company training is the loss of experience-swapping with delegates from other companies, and this has to be balanced against the cost saving.

Most of the well-known training establishments have facilities to organize this, but the initiative has to come from inside the company if it is to work. Every training venture needs an in-house champion to make sure it happens. The more senior that person is, the easier it will be to get it to happen. But you can start at any stage trying to convince your employers of the need for more training. Even if they refuse, they will be impressed that you want to improve your own skills and increase your own knowledge. They will be even more impressed if you can make the training an integral part of the company's strategy.

If, for instance, you want to lead the company away from above-the-line advertising and into direct mail and sales promotion – which you believe will be a far less wasteful and more powerful medium for the company's message – you will need to train everyone in the department, from directors to secretaries, in the benefits of direct mail, and teach them the fundamental skills required for writing direct mail letters and setting up fast response services.

If there is a particular skill lacking in a company, perhaps telephone answering skills or customer care, then a day or two's training for the whole staff will ensure that everyone is working to the same pattern and understanding the reasons for what they are doing.

Gradually, as you move up the corporate ladder, you will have more and more responsibility for training your subordinates, and possibly even your peer group and superiors. Only through constantly learning can a corporate team hope to develop and change to get to the forefront of their industry, and then to stay there. The same is true for the individual. Creating a corporate learning culture is essential for the long-term success of companies and the individuals working within them.

Anyone who is ambitious to develop themselves must have in their mind a clear picture of the skills they want to learn, and some idea of the time-scale in which they want to learn them.

They must then decide what skills they want those around them to acquire, because a manager will only ever be as good as the team providing the support and doing the work that will get the results.

In some cases you may even need to learn how to train others yourself, so that you can impart more clearly and coherently the way in which you want things to go. Being able to train and communicate is a useful skill for any manager, although there is a danger that if you are too good at it you might be diverted into full-time training instead of marketing – but then that might be a move you would welcome.

For training to be successful, however, individuals need to have 'bought into it'. You need to want to learn and you need to be able to see the practical use to which you are going to be able to put your new-found knowledge.

In many cases you may actually need less training than you first imagined. It may be, for instance, that an MBA course is rather like taking a steamroller to crack a walnut, when all you really need is a short course in finance or personnel, which could be gained at night school or on day release. Taking short courses like this along the way not only gives you qualifications from organizations such as the Chartered Institute of Marketing, but also helps you do your job better on a day-to-day basis. Qualifications gained along the way help to show how serious you are about learning to do the job, particularly if you do not have a university degree.

At the beginning of your career you will be in a better position to focus on the big training events, like the two-week courses, making sure that you go to at least one, and preferably two or three a year. In most companies these courses will be held at group level, but there will also be local ones and highly intensive ones.

In your first year you will probably need to concentrate on inter-personal skills, moving on to developing your marketing skills in the second year and business strategy and interviewing-type skills in the third year.

Traditionally there has been a wide gap between education and train-ing. Education has been seen as knowledge which is examined, and is now deemed to continue throughout life, not stopping the moment a person leaves school or university, while training is something given to help the individual to be better at their job as perceived by their employer.

The borderline between the two is now becoming fuzzy, with the National Council for Vocational Qualifications being set up to get all qualifications into a recognized format, standardizing them so that they can all be judged at one level. Delegates will be able to attend a number of short training schemes and still end up with a qualification by measuring their success on each, and they will receive a meaningful qualification at the end. Called the Credit Accumulation Transfer Scheme, points will be awarded for a number of different training schemes, providing a training record that delegates can carry around with them throughout their careers.

There is no doubt that qualifications will help people to get jobs, particularly at the early stages of their careers where they do not have a long track record to show potential employers, although pieces of paper which are merely certificates of attendance are less useful. Later in your career qualifications will be less useful than the demonstration that you are willing to take time to train yourself in new skills, even when you don't have to.

The UK still needs to develop a learning culture. As the pace of change increases in the world of work, the need for training increases at the same speed. It has to become continuous, both on and off the job. There is a tendency among the British to think we know it all. There is also a danger that employers will buy training wholesale, without thinking through the individual needs of their employees, giving them inadequate briefings and de-briefings, which leads to a great deal of wasted time and energy.

Some people are good at training themselves, having the right amounts of self-discipline and motivation, and there are a growing number of products on the market such as computer-based training packages, inter-active videos and distance learning schemes. Most require facilitators, and many provide telephone hot lines for students to ring and discuss questions.

There are so many ways of getting training these days that there really is no excuse not to be taking advantage of at least some of them.

Continuous development

According to the Institute of Personnel Management, continuous development is 'self-directed, lifelong learning. Continuous development policies are ones first to allow and then to facilitate such learning at work, through work itself.'

The argument is that all companies depend upon their people, and they will only grow and become more effective and efficient if their people are nurtured so that they can learn and grow. Employee learning, therefore, needs to be managed continuously – not specially and separately, but constantly. Training is a continuous process not a series of short-term expedients.

A company that wants to get the best from its people needs to have some sort of strategic business plan in terms of skills and knowledge needed from the employees. Managers must be ready, willing and able to define and meet the needs for training as they appear. These needs can't always be anticipated so there must be a willingness to accept changes in direction (part of continuous development).

Wherever possible, learning and work should be integrated, which means employees need to be encouraged to learn from the problems, challenges and successes they meet every day.

The impetus for continuous development always has to come from the top, and needs to be constantly reviewed. Investment in this is as crucial as investment in research, new product development or capital equipment. It is not a luxury that can only be afforded in the good times. In fact the more severe the problems facing a company the greater the need for learning on the part of its employees and the more pressing the need for investment in learning.

Companies are responsible for ensuring that their employees are being continuously developed, but equally individuals are responsible for their own continuous self-development.

Companies have to look into the best ways to teach new skills and enhance old ones, and they have to be prepared to acknowledge improved performance, using enhanced skills operationally and providing appropriate rewards.

The question everyone should ask themselves regularly is 'how long is it since I learned something new at work?'

19   *Continuous assessment*

Throughout your career it is important that you are constantly aware of what your employers think of your performance. People don't always say when they are dissatisfied with your work. If you don't check what they think of you it might be years before you realize that other people are being given the breaks and you are not progressing. Things may even be getting really bad but everyone is too nice to tell you, until it's too late.

There may be some obvious pointers to the fact that you are succeeding or failing. You may be given promotions and raises in income which you were not due automatically, in which case you can be fairly sure that someone up there is happy. Alternatively you might find that everyone around you is being given these things and you are being deliberately missed out.

If you are a marketing person you will be aware of the importance of continually finding out the needs and wants of your potential customers, so that you can adapt and tailor your products to fit. If you don't take the trouble to find out what the customers want, you will be trusting to luck that your products will find a market. It is the same in your career. Unless you are sure that you know what it is your bosses expect from you, and how they feel about the service they are receiving so far, you can't know whether to alter or fine-tune your behaviour – or possibly move on to an employer who is more suited to your way of working.

It is a question of building a rapport with those above you – and those below you who are just as dependent on knowing what you think of their performances. It is not enough to wait for an annual review, which will either be a cursory meeting or else a terrible shock when you discover that a boss you thought was quite happy with the way you were doing things turns round and tells you that you are not satisfying the company's needs and you will either have to shape up or get out.

Although we have said that the days when employees could expect to stay with a company throughout their working lives are over, there is still a need for loyalty on both sides while you are working for somebody. Loyalty only comes through openness and regular communication. Unless you can build a rapport with your superiors and a sufficiently open relationship which allows you to talk frankly, you are going to be working at a considerable disadvantage.

Don't allow them to get away with vague answers to your questions; get them to be specific about what they want you to do, why they have made certain decisions about what they are asking you to do, and how they see your future. It doesn't have to seem as if you are being pushy and trying to get ahead of the queue; you simply need to know where you stand all the time.

In a good employer/employee relationship there shouldn't be any surprises. You should never come in one day and find that you are being dressed down for a problem you didn't even know existed. Likewise you should know if you are in the running for a big promotion or award of some sort. If any of these things come as a surprise it means you haven't been communicating effectively with the right people on a regular basis.

Likewise your company needs to know if you are worried or unhappy about any part of your job. If you are not getting on with your boss, for instance, you should not let the situation drag on. The chances are that if you don't like your boss, he or she doesn't like you either, and that is going to slow down your progress. Either you will have to confront the person or, if that is not feasible, you will have to go to someone else, like your boss's boss or the personnel department. If there is a problem they will want to be aware of it, so that they can ensure that it isn't widespread (it may be that your boss is upsetting other people as well who are not coming forward). If they value your services they will find a way round the problem with you – if they aren't willing to do that then the time may have come to look around for a new job. It is better to be able to make a firm decision and act immediately, rather than let a bad situation drag on for months or years, and allow your performance to suffer as a consequence. The longer you leave a bad situation before talking about it, the lower your spirits will become, and the less likely you are to be able to make a good move.

If you are having trouble with the work, then you might need some extra training, or you may simply have taken a wrong turn and need to reassess where you fit in. Rather than continue to do a bad job, or feel dissatisfied with what you are doing, it would be better to tell someone and find a solution. It may be that when you talk to other people you will find that they are perfectly happy with your performance and don't see a problem. This may give you the confidence to carry on, and will alert them to the fact that they should be giving you more encouragement.

Whatever happens don't bottle things up, and do your best to make other people be open with you about their feelings and plans. Without information, either good or bad, you can't possibly plan your career in an intelligent way. It would be a shame if you thought you were unappreciated and went off and took an inferior job somewhere else, when all the time your current bosses thought you were doing a great job. Equally it would be a mistake for you to remain in a dead-end job for years, declining better offers elsewhere, because you are under the mistaken impression that your bosses are grooming you for better things.

Managers should be facilitators and encouragers so they should be willing to talk and listen, and you should always be made to feel confident enough to disagree openly with your bosses. It is important that you feel you can be honest with those above and below you, and every company has got to be prepared to give people room to make mistakes and learn from them.

Now that there is greater emphasis on the bottom line in business rather than size for its own sake, it is possible for companies to move responsibilities further down the line. It is up to individuals to ensure that they are given those responsibilities, and if they are not being given them then they need to know why.

If somebody is being developed for high office, their employers must be able to understand their motives for work, and this requires a continual rapport, with reviews and assessments being used purely for fine tuning, and for the setting of agreed objectives and goals for the next period. Catastrophe management and reprimands are the signs of a management system which isn't working.

All this supposes an ideal world, but of course in most companies the human resources issues get pushed to the bottom of the list, when in fact they should be right at the top. A company needs to anticipate if one of its employees is unhappy, and to understand why that might be. Employers and employees need to appreciate one another's efforts on their behalf – a formula for loyalty.

So make sure that you seek continual feedback on your achievements from everyone around you. It is vital that you get to find out how others see you, even if the truth is not as pleasant as you would like. It is often a shock to find out that others have a completely different view of you from the one you expect. But you need that objective data in order to make decisions on what you should do next – even if that is merely to set about correcting people's mistaken ideas about you.

You need to know conclusively what your strengths are. In his book *Managing Your Own Career*, Dave Francis suggests that from a careerist's point of view a strength has four aspects: the skill to perform well; the willingness to perform well; the confidence to perform well; and recognition by others.

The first three aspects you can control yourself, but for the fourth you are going to have to involve others. Without that recognition you will never receive the opportunities your talents may deserve.

If your self-image is badly wrong, because you have either over-estimated or under-estimated your strengths in the eyes of others you will be vulnerable to serious career mistakes. You may miss opportunities because you don't believe you are up to them, or you may take on tasks that are way beyond your capabilities and seriously damage your reputation as a result. You can only get an accurate picture of your abilities by talking to a wide cross section of people about yourself.

It is important, of course, that you are able to take criticism in a positive fashion. It is no good asking people to be honest with you if you are going to become hurt, deflated and demotivated by what they say. You need to concentrate on what they are saying to you and absorb it without jumping in with justifications for why you do certain things in certain ways.

It is also important that you find out what these people are feeling as well as thinking. Their subjective views of you are valid and important simply because they exist. Don't insist that they justify everything they say; the fact that they say it is enough. Later, while reflecting on what has been said, you can start to separate fact from opinion and make some value judgement on the information you have gained.

If they are raising important points then it would be a good idea to ask them to be as specific as possible, to give you illustrations of what they mean, so that you can be clear about where you are going wrong – or right. Ask them to stick to things that are within your control. It is no good being told about things that you can do nothing about.

If someone says something that worries you a great deal, get second, third or even fourth opinions. You don't want to change your whole method of working just because of one person's opinion. They may, after all, be wrong, or at least be in a small minority.

Career planning by companies

Some of the more forward-thinking companies are now providing support for employees with their personal career planning. Whereas in the past this was done by senior management telling people what they were going to be doing, there is now more recognition for the value of encouraging employees to plan individually. In some companies this sort of service is only available to people with specific career problems or in an 'outplacement' situation, but a company that puts a greater and more widespread commitment into the process tends to reap greater rewards as a result.

Employers are not doing this for purely altruistic reasons. There can be major advantages to be gained from boosting the morale of the workforce and making them feel good about themselves and confident about their futures, particularly at difficult times when a company might be laying a lot of people off, or merging with another organization, or simply not be in a position to offer fast-track career progression.

Anyone who is put through a career planning programme is likely to be much clearer and more articulate about what they are doing within the organization and why they are doing it, and they are likely to ask questions about the efficiency of the job they currently hold. The process will also open lines of communication between managers and the people they manage, forcing them to find out about one another's needs and plans. The company, therefore, will benefit as much as the individual, although that should not be the primary objective.

Companies that want to introduce this type of scheme need to be clear about why they are doing it and what kind of programme would be best for them. They need to plan carefully how to introduce and communicate it.

In most cases a career counselling programme will reveal that the majority of employees are happy with their current jobs, but during the discussions it will become apparent that for some individuals certain adjustments need to be made to their job specifications. It might be that an employee could handle more responsibility, or that they are being stretched too far in different directions and the job parameters need to be redefined. The idea is that the company should provide its people with the tools to plan and manage their own careers effectively.

A programme could be built around any number of different systems. It could include planning committees, succession planning, guidance for managers in coaching and counselling employees and workshops and self-study workbooks to assist individuals in their own planning.

Workshops can be useful in bringing together people from different parts of the organization, providing an opportunity for everyone to learn more about the company they work for and the opportunities it offers. The negative side is that some individuals may be reluctant to discuss their private ambitions and worries in a group atmosphere, particularly if they feel that other members of the group are their competitors in any way. In those cases individual counselling might be more effective if the company has sufficient resources.

It is important that the process does not become too much like a performance appraisal, and it should probably not be mandatory, otherwise employees will begin to believe that the whole thing is being done for the benefit of the organization, when it should in fact be for them, with the company merely benefiting from their increased commitment and raised morale. Management's role is to coach, counsel and advise, not to evaluate or judge the employees they are working with. The aim is to make individuals more self-reliant and independent.

20 The right time to go into consultancy

Spending some years in consultancy can be a good career development move at certain stages of a marketing person's working life.

Earlier we talked about the advantages and disadvantages of going straight into a consultancy at the beginning of a career. At that stage the pros were outweighed by the cons for most people. After four or five years of working for a blue-chip company, however, the advantages begin to increase and the disadvantages diminish.

Once you have laid the foundations of a career in a well-known company you can always go back later, either to the same company or to another of equally high repute. You have by then had the training, and hopefully the job experience, to prove that you are able to succeed in the 'real world'. You have also become a very tempting proposition to the consultancy companies.

When clients hire a consultancy they are doing so on the track record of the individuals who will be handling their account. If you can show that you have been successful in a company that is known to be at the leading edge of its industry, then you have an instant pedigree – you have experience the consultancy can sell.

For you the advantages are both short term and long term. In the short term you will be able to increase your salary by anything up to 100 per cent (50 per cent would not be at all unusual), and you would be able to broaden your experience from the first day.

In the course of a year a consultancy will be working for any number of different clients on a wide variety of assignments. Some of them will be very mundane, the sorts of jobs client companies prefer to land on someone else's plate, but others will be exciting, with the variety making up for the tedious jobs. You will get opportunities to deal with the top levels of corporate management, setting strategies and finding out exactly how different companies work. You will be analysing problems at the highest levels, covering the widest situations, and witnessing how senior people operate.

The variety and challenge of the work will be exciting, but it will also be a highly pressured working environment involving long hours and a great deal of travelling. If one client is in Aberdeen and another is in Portsmouth, those are the places you are going to have to get to. If an assignment takes several months you may find that you are virtually living away from home during the weeks.

Because of the pressure, and because it is such an intensified learning experience, consultancy is generally more suited to those still in their twenties or early thirties. It can play havoc with your private life, and someone who has heavy family commitments might find the strain unacceptable.

For someone on the way up, however, looking for excitement and variety, the opportunities are perfect. Consultancy work is multi-disciplined and multi-industry. It can accelerate career development by 100 per cent, but it can also double the workload. A decision will soon have to be taken, however, as to whether the move to consultancy is a temporary learning experience, or a lifelong career. If it is just a learning experience it is important not to stay too long.

There are several dangers involved in remaining in the consultancy world too long. The first is that before long your actual 'on the job' experience becomes a distant memory, and your CV begins to fill up with short-term consulting assignments. If you are flying high enough you may be able to win new business for your consulting company on the strength of the jobs you have been doing, but many clients are still more comfortable with someone who has had recent experience in a major company. As that experience drifts into the past, they begin to worry that you might be out of touch and out of date with what is actually happening in the real world.

It is possible that those fears are well founded since busy consultants seldom have enough time to go on training courses themselves. They are therefore living their whole lives in the rarified atmosphere of long-term strategy meetings with senior management. It is exciting work while you are on the way up, but it can soon start to appear divorced from the real world.

In the consultancy world the pressures are always on to win new business. You always have to have your eye on the bottom line, and that can take away some of the pleasure that you might be deriving from the work.

The next danger is that you will leave it too late to get back into a blue-chip company when you want to. If you spend three or four years in a consultancy you will have increased your market value considerably, and will be able to go back into the mainstream of business at a considerably higher level than the one at which you came out. If you leave it much longer than that, however, you will begin to seem a less attractive proposition.

People working in consultancies seldom stay inside the client companies long enough to see the results of their work coming through. They are not, in the end, answerable for what they do. In some cases they might make their recommendations and the client company might, for any number of reasons, decide not to act on them at all. After a while this begins to make someone look less attractive to a company that wants people who have a track record for seeing projects through from beginning to end, and taking the short-term downs with the long-term ups.

For the same reasons, many people find that, ultimately, consultancy work is unfulfilling. The consultants may be right in the middle of things and dealing with the most influential people in the client companies but in the end they have no real power, and that can be very frustrating as you become more senior. Before long, people who have worked in client companies become tired of always being the outsiders and long to get their teeth into a full-time job again. It may also be the case that they grow tired of climbing on and off aeroplanes and driving up and down motorways.

Some people, of course, thrive on the adrenalin and are perfectly suited to the lifestyle. They may go on to start up consultancies of their own and follow the entrepreneurial route.

Four out of ten marketing people probably dream about setting up their own businesses, but probably only two of them actually do anything about it. Although you need to have a sprinkling of entrepreneurial talent in order to succeed in marketing, it takes a great deal more to start up on your own.

Marketing itself is not a fundamental skill, it is not actually about buying and selling in order to survive day to day, and that is usually what setting up on your own is all about.

There are a number of management consultancies offering marketing advice. Some of them specialize just in marketing, and they provide good potential career patterns to people who want to remain in the consultancy world and climb to the top of it. The majority of the best-known consultancies, however, are parts of the large accounting firms, all of whom have branched out from accountancy into other forms of management consultancy, and have included marketing in their portfolios. These firms offer limited career prospects for employees at the moment, because the top positions in the companies are nearly always filled by accountants. The marketing arms are still very small compared with the financial and auditing sides, and it would take someone of enormously high calibre to make it to the top from a marketing start.

Although the long-term career prospects in consultancy are limited for anyone except the most entrepreneurial, however, the short-term ones can be spectacular. These companies generally have good reputations, and have access to all the biggest blue-chip organizations in the world. In fact the biggest ones are now so successful that they themselves have become blue-chip. Provided you have stayed for the right amount of time, their names will add another level of authority to your CV.

The consultancies themselves are not unduly concerned with the high turnover of their staff. First because they like to be able to bring in new people with good track records and up-to-date experience in the field, and secondly because ex-consultants nearly always feel an affinity with their old firms and give them assignments.

Often consultants go on to join the staffs of the clients they are consulting for. Clients who are pleased with the strategic plans a consultant has done for them may ask if the consultant would like to join them and become involved in implementing the plans for real. Similarly a consultancy doing a lot of work for a particular marketing manager may find there is a good rapport between them and offer the marketing manager a consulting job at the end of the assignment. There is a general atmosphere of give and take, which is good for the consultancy business, keeping it fresh and alive, and consequently good for the clients it serves.

If a consultancy keeps losing key people to client companies it will soon build up a network of people in influential places who feel a loyalty to the old firm, and who will be putting work in its direction.

The consulting industry needs people from every industry, preferably with several different jobs already under their belts. It likes people who can prove that they are able to deliver results and demonstrate genuine business achievements. Consultants have to be able to deliver answers, they have to be able to think on their feet and they have to be able to think laterally.

The positions in the consultancy world usually equate to the marketing profession as follows:

Product manager	Assistant consultant
Senior product manager	Consultant
Marketing manager	Senior consultant
Marketing director	Managing consultant

Associate directors in consultancies generally come up internally.

What do consultancies actually do?

Consultants will usually do whatever the clients ask of them, and the main needs for their services fall into a number of categories.

As Marketing Improvements Group explain in their corporate literature, clients are looking for objective, practical advice, based on proven industrial and commercial experience as well as academic qualifications. They are looking for people who are capable of understanding their industry, their markets and their organizations without the need for extensive briefing. They also need the specialist marketing knowledge necessary to devise effective strategies and the tactical skills to make them work in practice.

A company like Marketing Improvements aims to field a team of sufficient size, breadth and track record to meet these needs. All the members of the team will have worked with major enterprises and will be professionally recognized.

They aim to help clients to understand better the dynamics of their markets and the activities of their competitors, and to define and select more accurately high potential target segments. They can assist clients to plan a more competitively differentiated marketing mix of products, prices, distribution, promotion and selling, and to implement their plans more effectively through better communication with customers and better management and staff organization, training and motivation.

Consultants who are successful need to provide a synthesis of best current marketing practice and up-to-date knowledge of each major industry sector, and to employ experienced line managers.

All clients' needs are different, so every assignment is likely to be different, tailored to suit their current situation, likely future market and competitive conditions. There are, however, some main areas of activity into which most projects would fall.

Market research and analysis are services which all companies need at some time in order to understand their markets, customer needs, attitudes and purchasing behaviour, competitive activity, distribution patterns, and the effectiveness of current marketing activity, in order to provide key data for strategic and tactical decision making. For many companies it is impractical to do this sort of work in-house, since it is not a constant or predictable need. It is more cost effective to buy it in from outside specialists. Consultants are ideally placed for this kind of work.

Consultants can also perform marketing audits, using research, observation and discussion. They can report on the opportunities the marketplace offers and the threats the competitors pose. They can formulate proposals on how the client's strengths can be consolidated and how any weaknesses can be eliminated ensuring that marketing processes are genuinely customer-led.

Some client companies ask consultants to help them with marketing strategy formulation, evaluating how realistic their current marketing goals are and how effective their strategies. The consultants may recommend revised targets and may propose new strategies to achieve higher market share, new market entry, product development, diversification or increased profitability and productivity.

Consultants can provide product evaluations, assessing the performance of the client's products and services in relation to customer and trade needs and perceptions, with a view to recommending such courses of action as repositioning, product development or elimination, as well as the amendment of pricing policies.

The formulation of a cost-effective mix of messages and media is increasingly complex, particularly as communications systems and technologies are evolving so fast. A consultant can help clients to evaluate and plot their overall promotion, and especially to plan and implement their direct marketing and customer contact programmes.

Distribution is another key area, with organizations recognizing the need to 'market through' rather than just 'sell to' distributors. A consultant can analyse changing distributive patterns, helping clients to select channels and to manage and motivate outlets.

Consultants can also work with clients to construct better customer data bases and to utilize these to plan and implement product and promotional programmes. They can develop marketing planning systems for national or multi-national situations, and can establish monitoring and control procedures.

Organizations sometimes also need help with the tailoring of their own internal structures, to ensure that the marketing function and sales force are capable of effective planning and implementation. Consultants can define job responsibilities, personality profiles, reporting and communication lines, and advise on staffing, motivation and appraisal systems.

Many of the larger consultancies can also provide training and motivational expertise and resources for imparting attitudes, knowledge and skills through in-house training programmes, public seminars or distance learning.

Once they have made their analysis and recommendations, a consultancy would also offer to support the client through the installation and implementation of the plans, structures and systems, management and staff development, and may also be able to supply the necessary people, if required, on short-term secondment.

21   *Marketing services*

The marketing world encompasses a number of different disciplines, all of which come together to create the 'marketing mix' of communications through advertising, sales promotion and public relations, product design, distribution and pricing. Anyone hoping to reach the top as a marketing director of a major company is going to need to know something about all of them, and a lot about most of them.

Many of these specializations are largely, and in some cases almost entirely, catered for by independent suppliers. Advertising agencies for instance, have a virtual monopoly of the advertising business. If companies do have advertising managers, their task is usually to hire and then liaise with the agencies. In public relations and sales promotion the balance is more even, with a fair proportion of companies doing their own work. Market research and direct marketing are both areas which are served highly efficiently by specialist organizations.

A marketing director, therefore, may have jurisdiction over both in-house facilities and external agencies in all these areas, and since good bosses need to be capable of doing for themselves anything that they are asking other people to do, they need to pick up some skills along the way.

The most efficient way of doing this is by spending time working in the various in-house departments, learning how to brief outside agencies and oversee their work. Alternatively some time could be spent working in one of the specialized companies, although there is not as regular a flow of people back and forth in these areas as there is in the consultancy business. This would probably not be a move that many big-company people would make on the way to the top (unlike consultancy work).

Many people are attracted to advertising at the beginning of their careers, because it is surrounded by an aura of glamour. Once inside one of the agencies (and you will have to be good to get inside one of the big agencies), you might begin to feel that you would be happier to be on the client side of the desk. You might think that it would be more satisfying to be involved in both depth and breadth with a product, rather than just handling one specialized aspect for a number of different products at a fairly superficial level. You might also begin to hanker after the idea of being the one calling the tune.

Someone who has reached the level of marketing manager or director in a client company, and who has grown used to calling the shots on a big budget product as well as handling the overall management of the business, is likely to find advertising less intellectually stimulating or rewarding. Agencies are full of prima donnas and there are often tight deadlines which do not leave enough time for the work to be done as thoroughly as a client might desire.

Anyone in the service industries, and this includes consultancy, is at the beck and call of the clients. Whatever happens a client has to be humoured and kept happy; phone calls have to be returned and progress reports prepared. At meetings agency staff have to present their ideas, rather like school children handing in their holiday projects. The clients can then react with overwhelming applause, or dismiss months of work out of hand as being unsuitable. They might be lukewarm or discouraging, or they might want to make alterations which the original creative team believe will ruin the impact of their ideas. It is the client who has the multi-million pound budget; it is therefore the client who calls the tune.

There are always some high-flying agencies who manage to create such good reputations for themselves that they are able virtually to dictate to clients what they should do, knowing that if the client sacks them there are plenty more people lined up in the wings waiting to bring their accounts to the agency. These are the 'hot' agencies, usually quite young companies that have mastered the art of winning clients but have not yet grown big enough to need an overwhelming amount of turnover just to survive.

No agency, however, stays that fashionable that long, and eventually they are all back courting clients for business, and agreeing to do things they don't always believe in.

Anyone who wants to swap from the agency world on to the client side of a sizeable company will have to move quickly, while they are still young enough to go through the standard training mill. Their experience in the advertising world might be seen as useful work experience, but it would not be viewed as particularly useful training for general marketing. It is more likely that they would be able to move into a client company as an advertising manager, and might then be able to progress up into the mainline marketing department from there, but this would only work in a company with a relatively unsophisticated approach to marketing.

Well-established marketing managers in blue-chip companies however, might find it possible to move into advertising agencies on the account handling side and be very successful at it. But they had better be sure that it is a specialization they would be willing to stay with, because a few years in an advertising agency might make it impossible for them to get back into a blue-chip company on the fast track to marketing director.

For those who enjoy the more superficial and 'creative' elements of marketing, however, the advertising world could provide a more exciting and satisfying source of work than the client companies. There will be a constant air of danger and excitement, and there will be highs and lows as clients come and go.

Unlike the blue-chip companies, where you can predict with a fair degree of accuracy how many products you are going to sell next year, based on what you sold last year, an advertisng agency could have its turnover cut in half with the loss of a couple of clients, or doubled with the winning of a couple of new ones. Not everyone wants to be living with that sort of turbulence for long. Most advertising agencies tend to be staffed by young people, and unless the older ones have made enough money to retire to the south of France in style, start restaurants or go into the antiques business, they are generally left with a less than glittering number of options within the corporate world.

Public relations has been growing in importance and prestige in recent years, paticularly at the corporate communications and investor relations levels. For someone with a good sound marketing training behind them, some time spent working in the public relations department of the company, particularly the senior end of it, could be a useful stepping stone to a top position. Corporate advisers at that level are seen to have a broad and deep knowledge of the way the company works and of how it fits into the outside world. They have already proved that they have many of the attributes needed for top management, such as communications skills and a high degree of wisdom based on experience.

There might come a time when these people realize that they have got as high as they are going to get in their organization, and they might decide the time is right to move out into the PR consulting world. Setting up a PR company is a relatively low-cost business. Someone with a good track record in a major company will almost certainly be able to make a good living, and may even be able to grow the company into a sizeable operation, ending up by floating it on the stock market, or selling up for seven figure sums, providing they have the right entrepreneurial talents.

Those who have an entrepreneurial instinct might equally decide to go into the sales promotion, direct marketing or market research consulting businesses. If they are in a good job with a blue-chip company, they will probably find a supplying company who will be willing to take them on in the first place. Having gained some experience with that company they would then know whether they were suited to that field and could decide whether they wanted to stay with that company or use their experience to set up on their own.

Many fortunes have been made in all these areas, but it requires the right degree of nerve and hard work at the beginning, and the determination to build a business and not to remain closeted inside a big company.

In some cases the entrepreneurs who break away to form their own companies end up being bought out by the organizations they originally left, and finish up back on the board (a position they might not have reached had they remained on the corporate ladder all through their careers). But this is not a route to the top that can be relied on, and it would only work for someone who had natural entrepreneurial skills. It is as easy to go broke as it is to become rich in the world of start-up businesses.

While the people who are going to get right to the top of the corporate tree need to have a smattering of knowledge in all these specialist areas, those who are aiming at the management layer just below the summit could be well advised to choose a specialist skill as they approach the middle of their careers and make themselves exceptional at it.

To be the sales promotion supremo for Kelloggs or British Airways could be an exciting climax to a corporate career. To head up all the direct marketing operations for the Reader's Digest or American Express might make you almost as powerful as the chief executive sitting above you, and would probably be a great deal less precarious.

The prospect of 1992 and the unification of Europe has served to focus a lot of people's minds on the need to think of the whole world as a potential market, although the year itself is unlikely to witness any particularly dramatic changes for anyone.

It is just one more stage in a gradual evolution towards internationalism which has been going on since the invention of mass air travel, and which is picking up speed as it develops. Anyone hoping to get to the top of a major company is almost certainly going to need some international experience. By working in other cultures you will be able to broaden your outlook and give yourself more points with which to score over the opposition when you are in competition for new jobs and promotions.

British marketing skills are very well respected in other countries, and so anyone who has served a good apprenticeship over here is likely to be welcomed by a foreign branch of the company as a source of new ideas and energy. You will, however, have to make it known that this is what you want to do.

Some companies see the integration of Europe as an opportunity to penetrate markets they are not yet in, never having really thought about it before. Others see the integration as a threat to their home market, with foreign companies selling over here in competition with them, and are looking for ways to build their businesses in other countries in order to counteract any losses in the home market.

Product and manufacturing companies, particularly high technology sectors like information technology, are now seeing Europe, and indeed the rest of the world, as one whole market, whereas the service industries are looking at it as a series of local businesses linked together.

The best time to gain international experience is early on in your career, for all the usual practical reasons. It is harder to move from country to country when you have a family. Once you are settled in a new country with your spouse and children waiting at home for you, there is a greater temptation not to mix with local people to the same extent as you would if you were on your own – expatriate families tend to keep to themselves or to mix with other expatriates.

The important thing is to learn how things are done in as many places as possible, particularly in the markets which are strong in your industry. The more comfortable you can be in a variety of different cultures, doing business with a variety of different people, the easier your climb to the top will become. Someone who has achieved success in a foreign country has proved something about themselves which cannot be taken away. It is a mark of competence and is generally accompanied by an enormous self-confidence. It might mean working in America or the Far East, increasingly it means experiencing business in at least some of the European countries.

One of the criteria by which you would judge the company you first join would be by the likelihood of it offering you at least one overseas posting, if that is what you want. Anyone who has their eye on the top of the corporate ladder will certainly have to put in some time abroad.

Right from the beginning you need to let it be known that this is part of your plan. If you make it sufficiently clear that you are keen to travel, the chances are that the company will make an opportunity for you within a few years of your arrival. It doesn't much matter what the job is as long as it is in line with your overall ambitions, and as long as it will involve you in taking on responsibilities and getting to know your host culture.

The concept of 1992 and the Channel Tunnel has awakened a number of UK companies to the danger of their home markets being flooded by European companies who are willing to invest in sending their people out into the field. As a result the UK companies are starting to look around for people who are willing and able to go out and develop new territories for them. They need people who have already proved their abilities in the home market, and who are sufficiently entrepreneurial to survive in unfamiliar environments.

At the same time there are foreign organizations, from the Swiss to the Japanese, who are buying up British companies and looking for people to run them. Such organizations are going to be more comfortable with people they know will understand them and their cultures. If they are building international empires then they are also going to be looking for people who have shown an ability to move and adapt.

The historical problem has been the language barrier. The British have always been bad at learning other people's languages, and the situation has become worse with the general acceptance of English as the international business language. It has made us over-confident and lazy. We know we can 'get by' with English, so we don't make the effort to learn anything else. It is a dangerous attitude for anyone wanting to succeed in the international marketplace.

It is probably true to say that English business people travelling around the world will be able to make themselves understood in the offices and meeting rooms in which they will be working even if they don't have a word of the local language. They will, however, be left out the moment anyone lapses into the native tongue of the host country, either during a business meeting or at a social function like a lunch. As soon as that happens the English traveller is immediately at an enormous disadvantage. For a moment imagine how hard it would be to do business with a French company if your contact there refused to speak a word of

English, even when working in London. Imagine how impossible it would be to do business with the Japanese if they were as stubborn about learning our language as we are about learning theirs.

The European market in particular is fraught with cultural and legal complexities, many of which are impossible to understand without a basic comprehension of the languages involved. As the product differences continue to erode between countries, managing a brand is increasingly going to mean overseeing sectors which cover more than one country. Only those who understand the languages involved will be able to handle the jobs.

Because of the power of America in the world, and Britain's links with American companies and business culture, and because of the growth in activity along the Pacific Rim, the chances are that the British business community will, in the long term, 'get away' with not speaking other languages. In the short term, however, the costs are going to be enormous and anyone who takes the trouble to ensure that they are among the few who learn other languages will be well in the lead in the race to the top.

If you are selling to a potential major customer in France, and your competitors are also out there offering products, services and prices equal to yours but their marketing manager speaks fluent French, the chances are the customer will go for the company that has made the effort to speak the language and that he or she thinks will be the easiest to deal with. Why should the customer do battle with language barriers if there is a choice?

How good your grasp of the language needs to be depends on how dedicated you are to the task in hand. Whatever you learned at school will almost certainly not be enough. It might be enough for you to supplement that grounding with training in the business terms of the language, but it would be better to go further and deeper.

This is the sort of training course you are going to have to seek out for yourself. Having found the course you should then go to your boss and try to persuade the company to pay for it, or at least contribute towards it. They will almost certainly be happy to do this if there is already a job abroad lined up for you, and they will be understanding if you have always stated that it is your ambition to spend some time working in foreign markets for them.

If you have not done this groundwork in preparing them, you will now have to explain what your general strategy is, and why you believe it will benefit the company to help you develop your international abilities.

Anyone with ambitions to rise to the top in the next twenty years is going to have to accept that the whole world is now our marketplace, and that every company in the world is the competition. It will no longer be enough to excel in your own home town, and to excel in Europe you will need to speak the local languages.

23 Working for foreign companies

Given that we are all moving into an international business arena, it shouldn't matter whether the company you are working for is British, Dutch, American or Japanese. In some of the biggest companies, like Shell or Unilever, it won't matter what nationality the company was to start with, because they have become so truly international it is hard to remember where they originated. With smaller or more nationalistic companies, however, there can be some more obvious advantages and disadvantages to working for a foreign owner.

To begin with, you have to decide if you are going to be comfortable in the culture of the company. All nations have very definite ways of doing things, and however much autonomy they give to national branches during the good times there are always going to be times when things aren't going so well and the owners step in to take a tighter control of the reins. When that happens, will you be comfortable working for Texans or Japanese bosses? Are you comfortable in the different cultures of 'KITA' (kick-in-the-arse) management, or the 'everyone is equal in the factory' approach? For many people these provide ideal opportunities to work in ways which they enjoy and which might be hard to find in purely British companies. It is important to think carefully, however, about the cultural differences and what they are likely to mean in the long term.

American companies, for instance, normally have quarterly reporting, which leads to very short-term views of problems, and if your last quarter's figures were down you may find you are in trouble. The Japanese, on the other hand are willing to invest in the long term, with long pay-back periods but they tend to go in for arm's length final decision making, which might be a cause of frustration for many people.

Right at the beginning, when you are deciding what you want to achieve in the first few years of your career, it might become obvious that there isn't a British company that can offer you the right opportunities. If, for instance, you want to work for the market leader in a particular field, and that market leader happens to be American or Japanese, then that is the company you are going to have to aim for. Equally, if you have decided that you want to gain international experience in a particular geographical area, then it would make sense to choose a company that originates from the area of your choice, assuming that they are good employers and trainers and everything else about them is suitable.

Many of the major multinational companies work rather like the Foreign Office, posting their managers around the world whenever an opportunity arises. Once you have established yourself as someone who adapts to other cultures, the chances are that you will be moved regularly. Many American companies tend to think that anyone who is foreign to America will be able to cope anywhere else – in their eyes an English person is a European, and so could easily be asked to handle the Dutch or German offices.

To start with this might be appealing. One year you are in Europe, the next you are in South America – that will be exciting and challenging. It will also be a good grounding in the world of international business and the problems of cultural differences. It will be invaluable experience, often leading to you being able to take responsibilities that would not come for years in your home country.

By the time you reach mid-career, however, you might have grown tired of constantly moving. You may want to settle down and raise a family, either in your own country or in one of those in which you have worked. When that moment comes you have to look seriously at the opportunities on offer within your existing company.

Will they be willing to let you settle down? Or will they constantly be trying to move you on to perform again the miracles you have proved you can perform in the past? And if you are going to settle with one branch of the company, what are the chances of promotion to the position you want? Weigh up the pros and cons of your family growing up experiencing a variety of cultures, and the possible educational problems – different curricula in different countries, or UK boarding schools.

Many companies always appoint their own nationals to the top positions. If you are working for an American company in Britain, and you know that the managing director's position has been filled by an American ever since the company was founded, you are going to have to ask yourself whether you are willing to stay on a ladder where the top job will never become available to you. It may not matter; you may be quite happy to come to rest on the next rung down, and that level may be quite open to British managers. But if it does matter to you, you will have to move. You must decide what the chances are of your reaching the top, and possibly have a look round the marketplace to see who else would be interested in the enormous pool of experience you have managed to acquire.

24   *The big break*

A lot of successful people have one major break in their lives, an opportunity which presents itself at just the right time, and allows them to realize their full potential. For most people that opportunity arrives during their mid to late thirties, but it can come at any time.

The secret is to be able to recognize it when it arrives and to have done the groundwork to be able to grasp it. This is where you start to climb into the branches of Peter Needham's career tree, confident that below you is a firm trunk of solid experience and deep roots of training and skills. When you have ensured that you have all the functional and marketing skills needed, you can expose yourself to the risk of an offer that will advance your career this quantum leap. Even if you are not sure whether you want to make the last leap, it is worth finding out what your options are by looking around at the job market open to you. Although you can't predict exactly when this moment is going to arise, or what form it is going to take, you can go a long way towards putting yourself in the right place for good fortune to strike.

Let's assume that you have made all the right moves up to now. You are in your mid-thirties and you are in the upper reaches of middle management in a company with an excellent reputation. You have a track record filled with successes, perhaps with just that company, or perhaps with one or two others before that as well, possibly including a stint in consultancy. You feel confident and happy with yourself, and you feel that you would be able to handle something much bigger than the job you are currently holding down.

Start by looking around your own company. Decide whether you would be happy to stay there for the next stage of your career, and whether you are likely to be given the opportunity to move on to something really worthwhile. If you are unsure of your position, then ask the people above you. What do they think your chances are of getting to the top? Can you move up now? If they try to put you off with 'wait a few years and see what happens' type answers, then the time has come to look around at the rest of the world, and see what it has to offer.

Later in the book we will look at the various ways in which you can do this, and the people whose help you can call upon. At the moment we want simply to ascertain whether you truly do want to make this jump or not.

If, when you have taken stock of your situation, you decide that you don't actually want to go any further, that you are quite happy at the level you have reached, then you should feel no pangs of guilt or inadequacy. It is far better to stay in a job where you excel and which gives you satisfaction, than to move up purely because you think you 'ought to', or because you want more money. That way lies disaster, disappointment and ulcers. If you are unsure what your true feelings are, don't be afraid to go in search of help, either within the company in the personnel department, or outside with any of the various career advisory companies – which we will discuss in more depth later.

It may be that the big break won't happen for another ten years, although the chances become slimmer as you go along. The important thing is to be sure that you are happy with what you are doing. Now would be a good time to take another look at the goals you set yourself ten years ago and decide whether they are still relevant. If they are not, then you must decide what the new ones should be. If they are relevant you must decide if you are on-target so far, and how to get to the next stage.

If you have reached group brand manager or marketing director level in your company, and your bosses make it clear that you are unlikely to make the jump to the next grade in the near future, it may be that you need to take your expertise and move to a different type of company. If you are currently with an fmcg company, for instance, you could probably move to a service or consumer goods company as marketing director, with all the requisite increases in your status, earnings and responsibilities.

It is at this stage that people suddenly find they are equipped to take on a really big challenge, and at the same time they may be able to double their money and put themselves directly in line for a managing directorship somewhere. When asked what it is that makes them want to do their jobs, most successful people cite the challenge and the job satisfaction rather than the money. They usually passed the point where they had as much money as they needed for their lifestyles within the first ten years of their careers. Most go out in mid-career in search of responsibility and challenge. Not everyone can hope to get into the top jobs at the big, blue-chip companies, but the world is full of opportunities in other areas for people who have been groomed for stardom in these highly reputed operations.

Not everyone, however, is psychologically equipped to move industries at this stage of their career. If you have always worked for a highly professional fmcg company, for instance, you may not be able to cope with the difference in approach that you might find in a smaller, less well-organized corporate structure. If you have never had to think about 'cashflow' because your company turns over several billion pounds a year, you might be uncomfortable joining an entrepreneurial company that is flying by the seat of its pants, unsure whether it is going to be able to meet the wage bill for next week, let alone the marketing budgets for next year.

It is time to ask yourself some serious questions about who you are and where you have got to so far.

It is also important to ensure that there is enough room above you in the new company. As you get older it may become harder to change companies again, so you need to know that the option of staying put is available to you. This will mean that there will need to be at least two more promotions open to you in the future. It might be a mistake to take the very top job in a company if you are going to be there for another thirty years, unless you believe you can grow the operation under you sufficiently fast to hold your interest.

This is another stage where psychometric testing can be very helpful. It is critical, for you and for the company employing you, that you don't make a mistake. When you reach these senior levels there will be factors like share prices riding on the right recruiting decisions; you need to know that you are going to fit in before you take the jump.

25   *Quality of life*

There are some people for whom work is an overriding passion. Their one and only source of happiness is their careers. They love the challenge, they love the status and they love the money. Nothing else is as important to them, including personal relationships or even, possibly, their own health.

Many of these people will reach the top of their professions, but that doesn't mean you have to be like this in order to succeed. In fact such behaviour, if it doesn't come naturally, can lead to early burn-out and self-destruction.

If you are in a career, like marketing, which involves long-term plans and rewards, you cannot afford to behave in this way for long. Unless you have set up a company to sell your own product, marketing is not a profession where you can hope to have made a fortune by the age of thirty, after which you can retire to the south of France. When you are working for other people it is a marathon rather than a sprint, so you need to conserve your energies and spend them wisely.

For most people it would actually be impossible to work twelve hours a day, seven days a week without having a nervous breakdown. We might be able to do it for a short, sharp burst with no harm to our mental stability, but in the long term we have to have balance and variety in order to thrive and prosper as individuals. Fortunately marketing is not a career where these sorts of pressures should be necessary. If they exist then it is because the individual has chosen to live that way, or because the employer is making unreasonable, and foolish, demands.

It is all too easy, however, particularly at the beginning of your career when there seems to be so much to do and learn, and so far to go, to begin to believe that everything else should take second place to your career. Perhaps at certain stages you will need to concentrate on work to the exclusion of other interests, but in order to do that successfully you must have achieved a harmony and balance in the rest of your life. If you have a strong marriage and a supportive family, they will all be behind you when you take on a new challenge. If, on the other hand, you neglect your family for too long, they will begin to become disenchanted and will not be there when you need them.

Every so often it is important to perform a complete stocktake of your life, just as you should do a periodical reassessment of your career goals.

Ask yourself: how hard do I really want to work? How much time do I want to spend with my spouse? How much of a part do I want to play in the bringing up of the children? Do I want to leave it all to my spouse or to hired help, or do I want to be a major influence in the children's lives? How much time do I want to spend travelling? Do I really want to take another job that would involve moving house, taking the children out of school and away from all their friends? Does the family want to experience different cultures?

The answers you come up with will depend on your personality and the personalities of your families. Some spouses like those who marry people in the army or navy, are quite used to moving every few years. Others will be used to seeing the family breadwinner only at weekends, and then having to share them with telephone calls and paperwork brought home in a briefcase. Others will insist that family life is sacred and that going to work is merely a way of providing an income to support the home.

Many managers no longer live in the communities in which they were born or brought up. The working world has caused them to move away, either as single people or as part of a family. Relatives and old school friends are left behind. Those who are lucky enough to be able to build careers in their own home towns, or close to them, are going to benefit from strong roots, security and continuity for the whole family, providing a strong base from which the breadwinners can launch themselves into other things. Someone who takes on a job which involves them in being away from home for three or four months a year stands a better chance of succeeding if they know that they have left their family behind in a home where they are settled and comfortable, not living somewhere where they don't know anyone and probably won't stay long enough to put down roots.

There will always be times when it is exciting and necessary to travel to new places and undertake new experiences. For those who want to get to the top and be able to concentrate their energies on their work when they need to, however, it is important to have stable home lives for as much of the time as possible. In their researching of top executives and how they got there, Korn/Ferry International discovered that almost all really successful businessmen (they didn't find any women at that level), had only ever been married once and had stable home lives.

There is no doubt that domestic problems take their toll on careers. It might be better to make the effort to be home an hour earlier each day, and to arrange an extra holiday each year even if it is inconvenient to be away from the office at the time, rather than have to cope with the heartbreak of divorce or the strain of endless arguing due to your inability to put time into a partnership or family.

The important thing to remember is that, providing you are good at your job and have found the right niche or career track for yourself, you can control almost all these factors. If your company wants to move and you don't want to go, you can say so. If they insist that it will jeopardize your prospects if you don't go, and you still don't want to, that would be a perfectly valid reason to start looking around for another employer.

Sometimes, of course, it is going to be worthwhile moving, particularly at the early stages of a career, and possibly at a later stage when the big break comes along. If the company wants you to move, however, you are in a strong position to insist that they help you in as many ways as possible to make the transition worthwhile.

Moving homes is a traumatic experience for most people, even if the way is smoothed by the company financially, with bridging loans or other arrangements. Any employer who knows what they are doing will try to make it as smooth as possible for you. If you are having trouble selling your old house, for instance, which means that you keep having to travel back to it at weekends to mow the lawn and check the roof hasn't leaked, you are not likely to be giving your best to the new job. A wise company will therefore agree to buy the old house from you, knowing that you will be costing them more in lost performance than they are likely to lose on a house sale.

Often the most difficult choice is whether to move house, with all the disruption it will cause, or to commute long distances to a job but remain in a familiar home environment. There can be no one answer to this problem. If you think that the job is only for a short time, then it would probably not be worth uprooting the family, only to have to move them again in a few years. If, on the other hand, you are likely to be staying in one place for the rest of your career, the daily grind of travelling could take the most enormous toll on your energies and consequently on your performance.

Doing a life check

At certain stages of your career it is worth stopping and asking yourself some questions about your whole life.

Start by asking yourself what sort of person you want to be. Take stock of the skills, abilities, qualities and characteristics you have, and of the ones you would like to have. Strip away all the pretences you may have built up, and be honest with yourself. Who would you really like to be?

Next ask yourself what you want to do with your life. List all the most important things you want to attempt, achieve and experience. What sort of contribution can you make to the world as a whole person, not just at work, but outside as well? Take no notice of all the things you do because other people expect them of you, just ask yourself what you want to do, regardless of other people's demands.

Whenever you are offered a new job or new responsibilities it is always acceptable to ask for time to think about them before accepting. If someone tries to rush you into a decision they must have an ulterior motive. While you are deciding whether or not to accept the offer, ask yourself those two basic questions before any others.

Having decided on your basic goals in this manner you can then turn your attention to the actions necessary to attain them.

Ask yourself how far you have got to date. Write down everything that describes the current stage of development in both your personal life and your career. Put in the bad bits as well as the good. Are you fit? Are you bad tempered? Are you popular? Do you enjoy your family life?

Now that you know where you are, take some time to look back at how you got there. Look at all the people who have influenced you, and understand the various elements which came together to take you down the path you have chosen to follow. Again, be honest about the bad decisions and mistakes you have made, because they will have played an equally large part in making you what you are today.

So where do you want to go from here? What are you going to do today, tomorrow and next week to push your ambitions further along the road? This means being realistic about goals that are attainable now, and at ways in which you could prepare yourself for greater glories later on, such as learning new skills.

Look at all the things that worked for you in the past and decide how to make them work for you in the future. Look also at the things that have held you back and work out how to avoid them happening again.

You also need to know what you are going to do when you arrive at your goal. It is easy to become so involved in the cut and thrust of getting to the top that you won't actually realize when you have got there, and you won't be working to sustain and enjoy what you have achieved. If you aren't ready for this stage of your life you may find the attainment of your life's ambitions something of an anticlimax.

Finally you need to look beyond your accepted goals and aspirations and put them into the context of a larger picture, which will include what you will do after you have reached the top and after you have retired. This will help you to get everything into perspective and will give you a feeling of continuity rather than seeing your career as existing in a vacuum.

At the end of your life check you need to prepare an action plan which will set out the concrete steps you must take for each stage and the timings involved.

Maintaining your health

People have become much more aware of the dangers to health of stress, but all too often sufferers try to treat the problems once they have them rather than creating lifestyles for themselves which will keep them healthy in the first place. If you are even slightly run down you are not going to be able to perform as well as you should at work. This will mean that you fall behind and have to struggle even harder to keep up, which in turn makes you more run down, and so the spiral continues.

What happens is that there is suddenly a warning sign, usually in middle age, such as a heart attack or a telling-off from a doctor, and the patient wakes up to the fact that they are not exercising enough and do not have a regular or healthy diet. They then have to take drastic action, cutting out drink altogether, going on crash diets, jogging each morning before work, playing squash and all the other things to which their bodies have grown unused. Of course it is good to do these things but it should not have become necessary to take panic action, and whatever these people do now will not make up for the abuse they have heaped on their systems in the past.

It is as bad to eat too much as too little. Huge expense account lunches which leave you feeling tired and bloated are as unhealthy as sandwiches and packets of crisps eaten at the wheel of a car. Someone who wants to build a successful long-term career needs to take stock of every aspect of their lives, not just their ascent of the corporate ladder. If they are not leading healthy lifestyles they might end up performing less well than the competition, or they might even end up so ill and run down that they have to drop out of the race years before they have fulfilled their potential.

Only by listening to your body can you tell if you are doing the right things. Are you eating and drinking sensibly? Are you exercising a sensible amount, in quantities you can sustain forever, not in sudden bursts that can only last a few weeks or months at a time? Are you sleeping enough? Does your work make you tense and nervous? Are you having to take piles of it home each evening and at weekends? Are you getting enough holidays? Are you happy and physically comfortable with yourself?

How much money do you really need?

It is a cliché to say that people become trapped in their jobs, commuting daily to an office which offers them little or no job satisfaction, simply because they can't afford to do anything else. But it is a cliché which happens all too often. In many cases, however, these people could easily afford to change their lives for something more satisfying; they simply haven't thought it through from the right angles.

Everyone wants to earn more money. It is fun to have money and it makes us feel comfortable and secure. It is also a status symbol. Sometimes, however, we end up paying a price which is not worthwhile, simply because we believe that we need more money than we actually do.

It is also a cliché to say that 'money doesn't bring happiness', and there is no doubt that a lack of money can bring a great deal of unhappiness. We are not, however, proposing that anyone should throw up everything and join the great dispossessed underclass. This book is addressed to marketing managers who are able and willing to work at a number of different jobs, and who merely have to make up their minds what it is they want to achieve. If you have gained the right amount of control over your life you will be able to make these decisions and act on them, but you need to be sure that you are working with the true facts about yourself and your needs.

If you are earning £45,000, for instance, but you are unhappy in your work, there is little doubt that you could afford to take on a more satisfying job at £35,000 if it came along and still be able to eat well and heat the house. If, as a consequence, you were happier and more fulfilled by your new work, the chances are that you would be far more successful in your new job than in your old one, and your earnings would consequently move quickly back up to their old levels.

It might mean that you have to go without a holiday for a couple of years, cut down on the number of meals out, sell your boat, put off improving the house for a few years, or possibly even move the children from private schools into a state system. What sacrifices you have to make will depend on what your priorities are and how much you have managed to achieve so far. Doing this sort of 'what if' exercise doesn't commit you to making the sacrifices, it is merely a way of ascertaining where you stand, what your priorities are, and what your options might be. It may be that you could move jobs and earn more than £45,000 immediately and get more job satisfaction, but you may not pluck up the courage to take the first step unless you are confident that it won't be the end of the world if you slide down the payscale for a while, or even forever.

If, when you are doing this stocktake, you work out how much you need to survive at the most basic level, you will then know how firm a base you have for bargaining when it comes to a dispute of any sort with your existing company. If you know that you could halve your salary and still survive, they won't be able to bully you into taking a promotion or making a move which you don't think would be in your long-term interests. If you decide that you want to go home promptly at five o'clock each day because you know that you can complete your work by that time, but your boss always likes to keep meetings running until seven, you can't say anything as long as you are scared of losing your job. If, however, you know that if they cease to give you what you want from your working life, you will be able to leave and still survive, that will increase your self-confidence, put you in a stronger political position and consequently improve your performance.

For those who can manage it, it is good always to have the equivalent of your current salary in an investment account – that way you could last probably two years without another job. When you know this is possible, you can be honest with your boss without fear, and leave if all else fails.

Anyone who gives the appearance of being in charge of their life, and able to control their own destiny, is impressive. Employers need these sorts of people, and good employers will generally go out of their way to make sure they keep them. You can make yourself one of these people, but only if you are clear in your mind where your priorities are, and where you draw the line between loyalties to your employer, and loyalties to your family and yourself.

Personal achievements outside the world of work can enhance a CV, making up part of the pattern of a rounded personality. Likewise a personal failure, like a bad marriage, can be the cause of a bad career. A partner who doesn't agree with the way you are heading, or who undermines your self-confidence just when you need it most, is quite capable of sabotaging your chances of getting to the top. Someone who is bad at communicating with their spouse may also be bad at communicating with colleagues in the workplace.

Employers need to be aware of the dangers of promoting people beyond the range of their capabilities. The majority of people do not reach the top of their companies – there simply isn't room for them. This doesn't mean that they are all failures and the 1 per cent who get to the top are the only winners. It is important that we all identify the point at which we have reached our limits, and that once this point has been reached employers look for ways of enriching our jobs without promotion. They can look at areas like training, or add to someone's product portfolio, or give them greater control over their existing territory. There are any number of different ways of doing it.

This doesn't mean that companies should accept less than the best that people are capable of giving. It is possible to force people to grow by giving them a little more than they think they can handle. It can be a profitable exercise for the company and an exciting one for the employees, as long as they are not put into positions where a failure could do serious damage.

Having children

However much things may have improved for women at work in the last ten or fifteen years, they still have some much harder choices and decisions to make when it comes to balancing home and work. Men are still not expected to make as great a contribution to the running of a home as women, and ultimately most women feel that the responsibility for bringing up children rests with them.

With the demographic changes decreasing the number of potential employees during the 1990s, many employers are looking for ways of encouraging women to join them in the first place, and then to come back to them after they have launched their families. Many, such as Unilever, try to find ways of keeping women attached to them during the time they are at home with small children, by giving them part-time and freelance work which they can do in their own time. That way the employees don't lose touch with what is going on, and they remain interested in the world of work.

The TSB, as part of their equal opportunities programme, has introduced a scheme whereby anyone (male or female) can leave work for up to five years for a domestic reason, and will be guaranteed to get their job back at the same level at the end of it. A 'domestic reason' could cover caring for an elderly or disabled relative as well as for children. During this period away from the bank, the ex-employees will be offered part-time work wherever possible, and will be brought in for regular refresher courses to keep them in touch with their colleagues and with the marketplace.

All blue-chip companies are realizing just how valuable their people are to them, and in most cases are doing their best to make sure that good people stay with them. For smaller companies it is not so easy to make promises about holding jobs open for a few months, let alone a few years, since they have no way of predicting their employment needs that far ahead.

All employers, however, are now obliged to give women the statutory time off to have a baby. But who is to say whether, in a high-flying career, the woman will not slip back a place on the ladder during those months, simply by not being around when an opportunity arises? There is nothing a woman can do to avoid being away for at least a few weeks, and in most cases a few months, if she wants to have children, but this is only the beginning of the problem.

Women who might have been convinced that they would easily be able to go back to work and leave the baby with a trustworthy nanny suddenly find that it is more of an emotional wrench than they expected, and that the nanny is not as reliable as they might have hoped. The children get ill or unhappy, or, as they grow older, begin to turn the screws in the emotional blackmail machine.

Most employers will pay lip-service to being understanding about these things, but even in these enlightened times few are understanding when it comes to it. Someone, male or female, who is consistently seen to be having to deal with family crises during working hours will not move as fast up the corporate ladder as someone who can be 'relied on'. The only consolation women these days can take from the small changes that have come about in attitudes is that many fathers are also beginning to feel guilty about neglecting their families for work. Feeling guilty, however, is a long way from doing something about it.

Just at the time when all the major career breaks and experiences are on offer, the women are having to decide whether or not to have children. The men may be feeling guilty about putting the burden of childcare on to the women, but the overwhelming majority of them will still do it, justifying their decision by saying that they are the major breadwinners and so it makes sense for them to keep working.

The only way in which women can hope to overcome this serious mid-career handicap is with careful planning. At the beginning of their careers they must ensure that they get all the right training and preparation. They cannot afford to make as many mistakes as their male counterparts. They will then have to select a company that is helpful towards things like maternity leave, and do their best to convince them during the child-rearing period that they are still serious about their careers. Afterwards they can start on their way up again, either using company crèche facilities if they are on offer, or hiring someone at home.

The fact that so many women do so well in marketing suggests that it is a career which lends itself to careful planning and hard work. There is no escaping the fact that the women who want to have successful careers as well as successful family lives are going to have to work very hard indeed, particularly during the middle years. Many might decide that the rewards are not worth it and will drop out for ten or fifteen years in the middle. If they are talented they will still be able to enter the race again later in their lives, and will find companies who will be glad to up-date their training and set them on the career road again. Just when the men are coming to the stages in their careers when they may be starting to take it easier and coast on their past experience, the women are re-entering the arena, full of enthusiasm and ambition. Those who choose this path often stand a good chance of pulling back to the front.

Good employers know that gender is totally unimportant when you are looking for ability. Sometimes they will make choices simply in order to complement the existing mix of the team, but good people are scarce, and no employer can afford to ignore half the working population.

26 *Money money money*

At various stages in this book we have suggested that money shouldn't be the prime driving force in a successful career. If you get the rest of the equation right, we have argued, the money will follow on naturally. Jobs should be learning experiences, and it would be a mistake to frighten away an opportunity by haggling too hard over the money.

That doesn't mean, however, that money isn't important. Along with recognition, it is one of the major ingredients in job satisfaction and a contributor to all-round happiness. This is never more apparent than when you haven't got enough of it.

Most marketing people are concerned about being successful, part of which involves possessions and the status of earning good money.

Making money is good for your self-esteem, and the things that money can buy are generally enjoyable. Money is a major part of our culture of status symbols and is generally equated with power and success, although not always. The managing director of a major oil company or computer manufacturer may earn less than an entrepreneur with a chain of second-hand car showrooms. Both may get equal amounts of job satisfaction from their chosen careers, but there is little question as to who has the greater status in most people's eyes.

The point is that if you suddenly discover that you haven't got enough money to live comfortably, and that a lack of it is making you unhappy, the chances are that the cause of the problem is something deeper.

There are exceptions to the rule, particularly in non-market areas like the welfare state, where people are expected to work for ludicrously low wages because of the job satisfaction they receive. When it is a whole profession which is being undervalued and underpaid, then it is the money and only the money which becomes the point of dispute, usually with industrial action as a result.

Marketing, however, is not generically an under-paid profession. If anything, it is well rewarded in comparison to most. If, therefore, you feel that you are not doing as well as you should financially, there must be a reason specific to you. Either you are not getting on as fast as you should, or the company doesn't value your services as they should, or you have taken a wrong turn somewhere along the line.

Some companies do pay better than others, but are you sure that you have the abilities to get a job in a high-flying organization? It may be very annoying to find that your neighbour, who works for one of your competitors, earns 50 per cent more than you for the same job. If, however, you did your research properly at the beginning of your career, you will have been aware that his company was known to pay well, and you would either have tried and failed to get them to take you on, or decided for whatever reason that you would take a different course. Now you must rethink your plan if you feel that you are getting a bad deal. The first step may be to go to your bosses and find out why you are paid what you are. Find out how they assess your worth.

We all tend to notice the people who are paid more than us, even if they are only a small percentage of the marketplace, and we forget about the often larger percentage of people who are paid far less. It is right that we should be aiming for the top, but it would be wrong to feel constantly dissatisfied if there is someone somewhere earning more than us.

One of the ways in which employers can tell you that they are pleased with your performance is to reward you financially. That way they motivate you to perform even better and to make more money for them. If this isn't happening, you need to ask why not. Explain to your boss why you think you should be earning more, and ask why you aren't. If the answer is not satisfactory it may be time to think about moving on, or possibly moving sideways into something that will suit your talents more successfully.

People's financial priorities change radically as they move on through life. At the beginning you want little more than a healthy cashflow. You want to be able to get on with your work and be able to afford to lead an interesting social life on the side. A company can make a package look more tempting by including a nice car, and you may also be motivated by incentives like trips to the Caribbean as rewards for targets met and exceeded.

As you move up the ladder these things will become less attractive, particularly as you become able to choose and pay for your own holidays, although bonuses for good performance may still play a major part in your remuneration package. By the time you get to the £60,000 mark money is probably less of a priority since you are starting to pay heavy taxes on anything extra that you might earn, and comfort factors like first-class travel, better cars, insurance policies and generous pensions begin to seem more appealing.

People at the middle stages of their careers are generally starting to think about how to build up a lump of capital so that they will not always be completely reliant on income for their security. In most cases that means buying a property, and possibly putting more money into improving and upgrading it. The more ambitious start to consider the possibilities of starting a company for themselves, either from scratch or through a management buy-out, the less ambitious might be buying share options if their employers are offering these.

Then the priorities change towards thinking about pensions and the sort of long-term security which will allow for a comfortable final third of your active life.

For those who spend their entire careers in large companies, there is little they can do to change the basic pay structure, unless they move upwards to bigger or better jobs. Everything is carefully laid down as to who gets what at each level.

Many companies will try to lock people in, with perks such as mortgage relief and generous pension schemes. It is always tempting to take these sorts of enticement when they are offered, in fact you should take advantage of them, provided you are aware from the outset what it will cost you should you decide you are unhappy and want to move on. Changes in the law mean that you can now take your pension with you, so provided you do not get locked into the wrong scheme, employers cannot hold this over you. But even if that does happen, you must have worked out in your mind at what stages it would be worth leaving and when it would be a mistake.

If your employer offers you an interest-free mortgage, for example, you should accept it, but you would be unwise to use it as an excuse to buy a much more expensive house, a house you couldn't afford to live in if you were paying the normal market rates. If you do that, and then want to leave the company, you may have to sell up the house as well. That may not matter to you, but if you are bringing up a family and don't want to move to something smaller, it could be a uncomfortable transition. Alternatively you might become dissatisfied with your job at a time when the interest rates are high and the house is impossible to sell. That could mean that you are trapped in a job you don't enjoy by factors way beyond your control.

We have also talked about the big career breaks that tend to come along in mid-career, sometimes involving as much as double your previous salary, and possibly offering equity in the company as well. This is again a time to tread carefully. Wherever the rewards are substantially greater, the risks are going to match. If you are working for one of the big, famous name firms there are certain safety nets. Such companies may not be as safe as they were thirty years ago, but the chances are that they will not be going out of business overnight, and to a certain extent they will probably look after you whatever happens, even if it is only to give you a redundancy cheque.

If someone who wants to lure you away from this blue-chip employer is offering to double your salary and give you a stake in their company, it must be a much smaller organization. They are almost certainly going to expect you to work harder than you do at the moment, and there is always the possibility that the company will go under, with you on board.

There has to be a reason why they are having to offer so much money to get someone on board. The reason may be that you are a uniquely qualified individual and they will do anything to get hold of you. The likelihood, however, is that they know they are asking you to take a risk and they are trying to make it worth taking.

Whether or not you decide to go for it will depend largely on all the decisions we have talked about regarding quality of life. If you like the idea of another challenge at this stage, of the chance of making it really big, then you will take the opportunity and the money will come as your reward. If you are unsure as to whether you really want to go this far then you should not be swayed by the money, because if the money is all that makes you accept the risk, you will almost certainly fail.

Jobs that offer large amounts of commission and bonus should also be looked at carefully. It is important that there is enough basic salary to cover your living expenses, otherwise the company performance might drop for some reason that has nothing to do with you, and you will suddenly find that you can't survive on the money they are paying you. You will be forced into looking for a new job for the wrong reasons.

As you move further up the ladder bonuses become more useful because your basic lifestyle will not be affected if they don't come through one year.

Too much bonus is seldom desirable because it drives people to perform with short-term goals in mind, even if the business has long-term cycles. You can end up trying to pack business in before the end of the year and you could end up letting clients down by not being able to service that business effectively.

Any company investing in research and development and new plant will find it hard to provide yearly targets which are meaningful anyway, so often bonuses will be little more than pie in the sky.

27   *Developing a reputation*

The first secret of success is to be good at what you do. The second is to make sure that other people know how good you are, particularly the people who are in a position to further your career. That means the people above you in your own company, the people who work in other companies to which you might like to move, and the recruitment service industry, which includes the head hunters.

If you are good enough at your job you may, eventually, become known to most of the people who matter. They may never, however, realize the full extent of your abilities, and they may not be aware of you at the moment when they have something which would be a perfect career move for you. In order to make sure that neither of these things happens, you need actively to build a reputation for yourself.

This can be done in a number of ways, all of which will have the added advantage of helping you to develop the first necessity for success – excelling at your job. The next is to become an effective self-presenter. In the blue-chip fmcg companies most of the marketing people will be trained thoroughly in self-presentaion, being used to talking to a wide varieties of audiences. People who are marketing more complex and esoteric products, however, such as pieces of defence equipment, may be more concerned with the technical merits of their products and the way they sell them, and may be less adept at making good 'first impressions' on people they meet, and at promoting themselves. Whatever line you are in, you need to make sure that you are taking care of your own image and reputation.

The methods of developing a reputation fall into two main categories: speaking in public, and writing about your business. This may mean speaking and writing inside the company within the context of your job, thereby explaining what you are doing to senior management or to other departments either at intimate presentations or large-scale company conferences. Alternatively it might mean speaking on behalf of your company to the rest of the industry and to potential customers at conferences which are open to the public, or to invited audiences. At the highest level it might mean speaking and writing on behalf of your whole industry, explaining their views and actions to the outside world, through the press or television.

Most companies, when grooming people for senior management, will include skills training to cover things like public speaking and making presentations. It is important for anyone who wants to get to the top to take all the training on offer, and even to seek out more if they think they need it. Even if you don't use it for public speaking, the training will still help you to develop an air of self-confidence which will convince other people that you know what you are doing.

You can't rely on the right people approaching you and suggesting you write or speak, you will have to go out and actively court the publicity. To be heard talking at major conferences, and to be seen writing and being quoted in the leading industry magazines, are sure-fire ways of coming to the attention of the right people. They are also sure-fire ways of being found out if you don't actually have anything worth saying. If you are at all unsure of the information you have to impart, keep it to yourself. If you want to find out more about anything to do with your company or your industry, writing an article or preparing a speech gives you the perfect opportunity to ask questions you might not otherwise be in a position to ask. To be successful at anything, you can never ask too many questions.

Being active in trade associations and similar organizations will also help, first in making the right contacts, and second in broadening your knowledge base of the industry you are in and of problems besetting others in similar positions.

Some companies, of course, are averse to any sort of high-profile work on the part of individuals in their employment. They do not like to see corporate secrets gossiped about in articles, and will go to considerable lengths to protect themselves from having that happen. If you work for this sort of company it may be harder to find niches in which you can project your personal image to the outside world. They probably will not allow you to write articles for the trade press. They may, however, be keen to encourage you to speak at conferences. Every company has a vested interest in communicating with some target audience, and if you make it clear that you would like to do that job on their behalf, they will usually be happy to help you, provided they think you will be up to the job and will do them credit.

Try to find out what opportunities are available, and then let it be known that you would like to put yourself forward as a candidate. Never break company policy by publishing facts which the company considers confidential – such actions could bring the most successful of careers to a grinding halt. Find out who you need to get permission from, and then work out sound arguments to put to these people as to why you should be allowed to write and publish.

There will also be opportunities within the corporate structure to bring yourself to the notice of the people who can help you to move on, without having to resort to outside resources like magazines. There are almost certainly house journals and newsletters to which you could be contributing, and there is no reason why you shouldn't prepare reports you haven't actually been asked to do, and then distribute them internally, making sure that you take them to show your boss, with recommendations on what the company should do about your discoveries.

If you can demonstrate to the people above you that you are a skilled communicator and able to think broadly and strategically, while at the same time able to carry out the necessary tactical jobs, they will start to recommend you for other communications tasks. All the time you will be building up your store of information on how the business ticks, and where it is likely to be going.

As soon as the company begins to recommend you for other communications tasks, you can ask for extra training in whatever area you feel you need it. If you are unsure of yourself on stage then you need help with your presentation and public speaking skills. If you are going to be talking to the media you may need help in how to deal with interviewers and cameras. There are a number of courses on how to write articles, should you be finding it hard to create the right structures. You might also need training in crisis management. If you are going to be the company spokesperson when something goes dramatically wrong, you want to be confident that you do yourself credit when under pressure, and don't simply get used by the people above you as a useful person to shoulder the responsibility.

When something goes badly wrong for a company, perhaps someone poisons a consignment of chocolate bars, or an aircraft crashes due to a mechanical fault, the natural reaction of most people within the company concerned is to run for cover. They want to make sure that they are not held responsible for any of the consequences, and that they are not available for comment to anyone outside the company. In fact it might be a better career move to demonstrate just how well you can handle a crisis of this magnitude. Everyone in the business world knows how hard it is to be sitting in the hot seat with a hostile media and public firing accusations, and they will all admire someone who handles the situation with firmness, tact and dignity. However, to be able to cope in such extreme circumstances requires specialist training for most people.

If your company is happy for you to write for and talk to the media, you should draw up a small marketing plan for yourself. Decide which are the trade and professional magazines you would like your name to be appearing in, and then get in contact with the relevant editors. There will probably be three layers of titles which are of interest to you. First there will be the publications which are relevant to your industry (*Grocer, Retail Week, Travel News, Plastics and Rubber Weekly*, or whatever). Then there are the general management publications (*Business, Director, Management Today*, etc.), and finally the marketing and specialist trade press (*Marketing Week, Marketing, What's New in Marketing, Promotions and Incentives*, etc.).

You need to find out the names of the relevant editors, features editors and special features editors. You then need to approach them with ideas for articles that you could write for them (or better still with an article you have already written).

If possible, get to meet them so that they remember you, and keep sending them new ideas for articles that you could prepare for them, or that they could have written, with you as a source of information and quotes. If you prove to be a reliable source of copy (don't promise articles unless you are sure you can deliver them by the deadlines the editors set, otherwise they will stop using you very quickly), they will keep on coming back to you for more.

Although the primary motive for undertaking these sorts of exercise is to further your own reputation, they will also help you to do your job better. In order to write or speak on your subject you will have to stop and reflect on what it is that you and your company are doing, and try to work out what it means to a wider audience. You will need to do research, which will help you to broaden your own understanding of your business, and you will be forced to defend your point of view if other people disagree with it. All this is excellent experience and practice for anyone planning a career in top management, and something which you might otherwise not take the time to do.

Any exposure you get in the press or on the platform will give your company's name exposure as well, so it will be able to share in the credit, and will benefit from any business that comes in (particularly if you are in the consultancy business) as a result of your words. This gives the company a reason to encourage you to do as much as possible. You will also be meeting potential customers and potential future employers at conferences and seminars, building up your network of contacts for both personal and business use.

You can approach speaking engagements in the same way as article writing. Find out who the major organizers of seminars and conferences are in your industry and let them know that you are keen to speak and that you have a lot to say. They may also want to see some evidence that you are able to hold an audience's attention and give worthwhile information. That can be something of a Catch 22 situation for anyone who is just starting out. One way to break in is to invite the organizers of the conference at which you want to speak to hear you talk at some in-house function or smaller venue. It is a question of building up your reputation step by step, making sure that everything you do leads on to something else.

Writing reports and doing research for internal consumption could lead to the material being published in a magazine at a later date. If you are having articles published in the trade press, you have something tangible to show to the seminar organizers.

If you find that this sort of reputation-building exercise suits you, and you are comfortable talking in front of audiences and cameras, or able to write fluently and quickly, there are any number of ways in which you can develop your skills. You could move towards becoming a general media spokesperson for your company, or you could move towards writing books on your subject.

There is a danger, of course, that these sorts of extra-curricular activities become so time consuming that you begin to neglect your real job. It is also possible that they will begin to pay you as much money as your salary. You will then have to decide how to balance them so that the work you are employed to do gets done, and you continue to build your reputation while at the same time not losing sight of your basic objectives.

28 Networking

'Networking' is a popular buzzword in executive recruitment circles, although not everyone who uses it can actually come up with a definition when challenged. Those who can define it have widely varying ideas.

On the whole, most people seem to understand it as meaning much the same as the 'old boy network', but used more proactively.

It most often comes into play when someone finds that they suddenly need a job because something has gone wrong with their current employment. They may have been made redundant, or they may just feel unhappy wherever they are and want to move. For some reason they need to find something fast, and have to explore every possible avenue as quickly as possible. That is when they will start to think about what sort of network they might have built up in the previous years that will help them now.

Few of us consciously build networks as we go along, and most of us would deny that we actually possess one if we were asked to produce it out of the blue. All of us, however, have one of some sort, and it is almost certainly more widespread than we first think.

During your career you will have got to know a number of people, many of whom you will have got on well with. Some of them will be well aware of your strengths and weaknesses because they have worked with you over a period of time; others will be less aware of what you have done, but having met you on at least one occasion will know you are a decent enough person and will feel obliged to help you should they be called upon to do so.

Some of these people might be old work colleagues who have moved on to other companies. Some might be personal friends, relatives or neighbours who are in positions relevant to your career. They might be old customers or old suppliers, or they might be competitors with whom you have worked for one reason or another. Each of these people knows other people, and that is how a network spreads out to become an intricate cobweb of opportunities.

There is an old saying that success is a question of 'who you know and not what you know'. This is patently untrue and is usually put about by people who are justifying why they themselves haven't been successful. If you are not good at your job no amount of 'contacts' are going to be able to help you to succeed. If, however, you are good at what you do, you will be able to offer something worthwhile to the people you know and they will be able to help you in return.

The British as a nation are still reluctant to use networking for a number of reasons. Some of us feel embarrassed to admit that we are looking for jobs at all. We are also afraid of being thought to be begging or asking for charity. On top of that is the fear that we might let down our contacts by turning out to be less capable of doing the job than we said we were. If a contact does help in the job search, there is a further fear that we will then be indebted and will, perhaps, endanger the friendship which existed previously.

Career adviser Roddy Braithewaite, when counselling people who are looking for new jobs, finds that many are reluctant to use networking, seeing it as undignified to admit to other people that they need their help and advice. He claims, however, that those who try it are amazed by the results. One man he talked to started off being adamant that he could never do anything like that, and had to be talked into it. He then became so keen on the idea that he started striking up conversations with complete strangers, until he met a man on a train who offered him a senior position in his company, simply because he had let it be known that he was looking for something.

When you sit down and work out how many people you have met in your business and social lives, you will almost certainly surprise yourself with the length of the list. The only criteria for getting on to the list is that people will remember who you are when you ring them. When you talk to them you can briefly outline your position and explain what help and advice you need from them. The likelihood that they will have something tangible to offer you at the precise moment at which you need it is slight, but they will almost certainly be able to give you three or four names of other people they know who might be useful, and will probably be more than happy to contact those people on your behalf and set up a meeting if relevant. If those three or four people lead to another dozen, the chances are that at least one of them will have something to offer you.

If you ask everyone you speak to if they know of at least two other people you could talk to, you will soon end up with a very wide network of contacts. Somewhere along the line you are bound to come across someone who has a need for the services you are offering. All you have to ask for is advice, so you don't have to embarrass yourself by asking for a job directly, or put the other person in the difficult position of having to turn you down.

You don't necessarily have to have a problem for a network to be useful to you. If there are a lot of people who know about you and your work, it is more likely that your name will be put forward to a headhunter who is looking for someone to fill a job that would be a perfect career move for you, or even that your name will be mentioned direct to an employer. It is up to you, however, to keep your list up to date and alive.

In an ideal world you should build a list of useful contacts as you meet them, adding on everyone you come across who impresses you and who looks as if they are going places themselves. You should then keep in contact with them in some way. It is unlikely that the contact will be regular, it might just be a Christmas card or a telephone call once a year to check that they are still working in the same place as when you met them, and to find out what has been happening in their lives. This is something many people find very hard to do and obviously you can't devote too much of your time to such speculative work, but the principle is sound since you never know when you are going to be talking to the person who will give you your next break.

As well as helping to increase your own personal safety net of contacts, such activity will also keep you apace with what is happening in other companies, and may lead to you making contacts and discovering information that will be useful to you and your employers. You might, for instance, discover that a particularly effective salesperson from one of your suppliers is unhappy in his or her job, and you might be able to persuade this person to join you. You might discover that a lapsed customer is now unhappy with the service he or she is receiving from one of your competitors and would be receptive to a new business pitch from your company.

No one can do anything in life without information, and most useful information, even in these days of high technology communications, is still carried by word of mouth. The more people you talk to and listen to, the more likely that you will be furnished with the most up-to-date and useful information.

A large proportion of interesting jobs are given to people the employer has met at some stage and been impressed by. The more people you get to meet the more likely you are to be talking to the right person at the right time.

The whole social world of business runs on the principle that you can't have too many contacts, otherwise there would be no earthly justification for the vast amounts of money and time that are spent on business entertaining.

Be aware throughout your career of the people you are meeting, and make sure that they remain aware of you.

29 Blockages

Blockages can and will happen at all stages of your career. They are always surmountable or avoidable, as long as you recognize that they exist and are prepared to do something about them.

Some may happen very early on and will be caused by the fact that you simply are not equipped to follow your first choice of career. If you don't have the talents to pursue the area you are interested in you will soon find out, and you can then look round for other ways of getting the same satisfactions using the talents you do have. At this stage you may not even be aware that you have reached a blockage; you may simply think that it is taking longer to get started than you first imagined.

As you go along you may find other factors entering the equation which you didn't anticipate. Your health may not be good enough to maintain the necessary workload for success. You may find that the social class or gender to which you belong is discriminated against in your chosen field or company. The discrimination may take such subtle forms that you are not initially aware of it, you just find that you are not progressing as fast as other people and no other explanation presents itself.

A lack of education may act as a barrier at certain stages, but there are usually ways round this through training schemes, if you are prepared to make the required effort.

Ageism can be a problem in the marketing profession. In fact some experts believe it is more of a problem than sexism. There is a general trend for fast-moving marketing executives to be thirty-five or under. Recruitment consultants find that anyone who is thrown out of work after that will have difficulty getting back in unless their track records are outstanding. It is an illogical situation, since experience should be at a premium in an industry that is developing so fast, but it is certainly a reality.

It may be that you live in an area where there are few opportunities of the sort you require, and you will have to decide whether to move to a new area or accept something less than you originally hoped for. Equally you may have other commitments which make it hard to give 100 per cent of yourself to your work – an invalid in the family who needs constant care, for instance.

Some blockages may be self-imposed, caused by your own failure of initiative, self-confidence or imagination; others may be nothing to do with you, but will require you to take the initiative to overcome them.

It may be that right at the beginning of your career you notice that everyone else from your intake of graduates or recruits is getting promoted and you aren't. This should ring warning bells, not only because you are standing still but because the more people who move ahead of you the harder it is going to be to push your way through.

You are going to have to talk to your employers to find out why this is happening, and you need to do some serious analysis of your situation. If all your peer group are better than you, it may be that you should think about moving on somewhere else. Of course it always pays to associate with the best in the business, and you will learn much more by working with these people than you would if you were among your own equals or inferiors, but from the point of view of your personal career path, you are unlikely to succeed in a company where you are below average as a performer.

You will have benefited from the training and grounding they have given you, but you might be wise to move on to something else before it becomes obvious on your CV that you have been left behind.

It may also be that you have a boss who is the same age as you. If that is the case you have to think very carefully about whether to stay or go. If, for instance, the boss in question has only just been given the job, the chances are that he or she will not be moving on for some time. This means that you will not be able to move up into their shoes. If you are looking to move in the short term then you will have to admit that this is a blockage. You might be able to sidestep it by remaining within the company but moving to another department, or you might decide to go elsewhere and perhaps come back to the company later, with more to offer them in the way of experience. Alternatively, you might decide that your boss is going right to the top and that if you can just wait a year or two you will be able to follow him or her up.

It is possible to become blocked because you are just too good at your job and your company does not want to move you for fear that it will find no one else to fill your shoes. If this is the case, and you are sure that you do want to move on, you will have to find ways of suggesting how you could continue to fulfil the tasks you are being given now, while delegating away some of the ones that could easily be done by other people, and adding new ones to your portfolio to replace them.

The most common time for blockages to occur, however, is towards the end of a career, when someone is believed to have reached the peak of their potential and is left to 'serve their time' until retirement.

In Japan they call these people 'window watchers'. They have been stripped of all responsibilities, their offices have been cleared of all paperwork, but they will never be fired. So all that is left for them to do is to watch the windows and draw their pay cheques at the end of the month.

It may be that there is only a short time until your pension rights mature, in which case you might decide that you would rather serve out this time than jeopardize your retirement income. You might even be quite happy to drift for a few years, having worked hard all your life. If, however, you find the situation frustrating and you are itching to do something new, meet some challenges and perhaps move further up the ladder, then you should not let the purely financial considerations of the pension deter you from making a move. It would be better to risk losing a bit of pension and living a happy satisfying life, than spending two, five or ten years enduring a demoralizing frustration, a state of mind from which you may never recover even when you have retired from the company.

Family firms can be particularly difficult for outsiders to rise to the top in if there are enough members of the family around to take all the top jobs. Mergers can also cause major blockages if there is a lot of overlap of talent at senior levels.

The important thing is always to be aware of the potential blockages around you. Continually ask yourself 'what if' questions: 'What if I don't get another promotion this year, when will the next opportunity come along and will I still be young enough to be eligible?' 'What if none of the people above me leaves in the next ten years. Will I be too old to get a worthwhile position after that?' 'What if I were fired tomorrow, would I be a good bet for a potential employer?'

This way you will be prepared for most eventualities. There will always be some events that will take you by surprise or will creep up on you so slowly that you don't notice they are there, but if you keep questioning what you are doing and what it is leading to, you will at least be able to spot problems in the early stages and begin to plan evasive action immediately.

If you find that more and more of your responsibilities are being taken away from you and given to junior people, but you are being given nothing new to replace them, now might be the time to start thinking about moving, or at least asking your employers what is happening. Don't wait until the last moment, because then it might be too late to do anything constructive about it.

30 *Selection consultants and headhunters*

The headhunting profession still has a number of critics. It has not been around all that long but, as with most fledgling industries, the sheep are now separating out from the goats, and the companies which are able to provide consistent and efficient services to their clients have grown and prospered. As the strong players in the marketplace emerged from the pack they became anxious to differentiate themselves from the others, and so acted with an even greater degree of professionalism and scrupulousness than might have been expected of practitioners in a more mature industry. They now prefer to be called 'executive search consultants', but everyone still calls them headhunters.

Their hard work has paid off, and there are now hardly any major companies in the world who have not, at some time or another, used the services of one or more headhunting firms to fill senior vacancies. Many companies use them all the time.

Now that the profession has become established (not that there aren't still some companies which provide a less than professional service, but they are shrinking to a reasonable minority), it has become a status symbol to be 'headhunted'. All too often, however, when you hear someone claim that they were 'headhunted' for a job, they actually mean 'recruited'; real headhunting is still only practised when looking for people earning over £40,000 or £45,000 a year, and in the majority of cases the money involved is probably starting at double that, going up to the sort of heady sums you read about in the annual reports of major companies.

Of course it is flattering to be courted by the big headhunting firms; it shows that you have reached a level at which you have become a desirable commodity, and jobs are chasing you rather than the other way round. It is also one of the major methods of getting into the top rungs of senior management. So how do you get yourself known to headhunting firms?

The answer is that you probably don't. In most cases you will just have to do everything else right and wait for them to come to you.

If you are not completely happy with your job and your current employer, you might be tempted to 'put yourself in play' with the headhunting firms. In other words, you might like to let it be known that you are available for offers. If you are not careful, however, you will immediately devalue yourself by putting yourself in the position of chasing them rather than the other way round. Nobody values something they can acquire easiliy as much as something they have to chase after.

If, however, you are sure you want to move and no headhunters seem to be coming after you, it might be worth sending round a letter with a CV to all the firms you know about. It might just be that your letter lands on their desks at just the moment when they have the perfect job for you. The chances of that happening are slight, but it only has to happen once, and for the amount of time it takes to send out a letter the odds are worth taking. If you are a particularly interesting individual (i.e. you are already demonstrably successful and in the right salary range), they may ask you to come in for a chat. Alternatively they may simply feed your details into their computers and promise to come back to you should something suitable arise. The odds are against anything happening after that, but you never know. By sending out these letters you are indulging in a sort of networking, and no effort is ever completely wasted in these exercises.

It would be much better in the long run for you to concentrate on doing your job well and on building your reputation, and to wait for the headhunters to come to you with their offers.

When a client wants to hire someone senior they start by calling the headhunter in to discuss their needs. Together they will work out an exact idea of the demands the job will put on the incumbent, and then begin to analyse what sort of experience will be needed to equip someone for the job. There will not be one career path only which will make a candidate suitable, but there will be certain ingredients which are necessary simply to be able to do the job. It might be that experience of heavy industry or the retail trade is vital, or experience in a particular foreign market.

The headhunters then go away and compile a list of people who could possibly fit the bill with their background and current position. They will get those names from their databases, and from research among everyone and anyone they can think of who isn't for some reason in the database.

By the time you have reached these sorts of levels in your career you will have come to the notice of a number of people in your company and in your industry. If you have been actively building your reputation through speaking and writing, you will have broadened that circle. When one of the powerful headhunting companies begins asking around, your name is likely to come up.

You may get an initial call from a headhunter asking if you know of anyone who might be suitable for the job; as the conversation progresses it will be suggested that you might think about it yourself. Alternatively they might just ring and ask you in for a meeting or a lunch, and decline to give any details until they actually meet you.

It is hard for most people to turn down such invitations, and it would probably be a mistake to do so. Even if you are happy in your current job and not intending to make a move, it is always worth knowing what else would be on offer should anything go wrong where you are. If you know that other people want to hire you it will boost your confidence and increase your bargaining power within your own organization. If you are currently a marketing director and another company wants you to become its managing director, you might be able to use this to persuade your company that it is going to have to do something better for you if it wants to keep you.

By talking to headhunters you get a chance to answer a few of the 'what if' questions that you should be asking as you go along through your career. You will be able to find out what sort of job you might be able to expect if you were to fall out with your current employers. You might also be able to find out your financial worth at the same time, although most headhunters prefer not to talk money until the end of the negotiations, believing that if they find exactly the right person for the job, the client and the recruit are more likely to be able to reach an agreement about money.

When they talk to candidates for a job, headhunters are looking for a number of fits. They are looking first for a technical fit, to ensure that the candidate actually has the experience and the technical abilities necessary to do the job. The chances are that they will be able to discover this fairly quickly, they may even be able to tell accurately before they meet the individual in person.

Next they are looking for a career fit, ensuring that the move would fit in with the candidate's career plans and patterns. It is no good offering someone a managing directorship in a heavy industrial company, if they are planning in the long term to become part of the senior management team in an fmcg company, for instance. There could be any number of subtle reasons why the job on offer would not be a good career fit, including personal reasons like the location of the employer or the potential workload.

Finally, and most importantly, they will be looking for a cultural fit. Will the candidate be happy working for the company in question? If, for instance, the candidates have spent all their working lives in the heavy industrial sector, dealing with people at factory floor and construction site level, are they going to be happy working for a computer company where everything happens in air-conditioned offices, or are they going to be happy in a home furnishings company surrounded by people who know more about colour matching and fabric swatches than heavy-duty lifting gear?

It is quite possible that a change of industry would fit well with the technical and career needs of a candidate, but that they simply wouldn't be comfortable in the new working environment.

It is also quite possible to change countries when headhunted, since many of the searches, particularly at the most senior levels of industry, are international. If they are looking for a marketing director for a soft drinks company, or for an aerospace manufacturer, the candidate with the right experience is just as likely to be in Britain, America, France or any other developed country. There have been a number of appointments in recent years which have crossed European boundaries, and that trend is likely to increase as more senior managers appear who have had international experience on the way up.

Good headhunters then have a vested interest in not wasting the client's time. If you are obviously not interested in the job, they should not try to talk you into it. Unless the client has told them to do everything they can to win you over, they should move on to someone else who is keener. Nothing could be more embarrassing for a headhunter than to place a candidate with a client, only to have him or her leave a few months later because the fit wasn't right after all.

The problem in most headhunting assignments is that the people who are the best for the job are already successful individuals. In most cases this will mean that they are perfectly happy working where they are, and unless they are caught at exactly the right moment with exactly the right offer, there is no reason why they should want to move. The people who most want to be headhunted are probably not enjoying the same levels of success and consequently will not be of as great a value to the clients. It is precisely these problems which have led to the growth of the headhunting industry. If it was easy to fill top jobs the clients would be doing it for themselves, not paying vast sums out to third parties.

So the best way to attract the attentions of the headhunters is to do a good job, and to build up the sort of track record that companies are going to want. At the same time you need to be networking and building your reputation to ensure that they have heard of you when the right break comes along. If you can't wait for this to happen then there is no harm in contacting them and letting them know that you would be interested in offers, but only view this as providing an outside chance of success.

31   *Career development advisers*

There is an enormous amount of confusion in the marketplace as to exactly who does what in the career advice business. The confusion is fuelled by the fact that a number of players are patently not providing the services they claim they are providing, although possibly in some cases they believe themselves to be genuinely useful.

The first differentiation is between outplacement and career counselling. Outplacement is always paid for by the companies concerned when they terminate employee services. They use the help of outplacement agencies to train employees in how to look for and win new jobs. Career counselling on the other hand can be paid for by the individual or the employer and is aimed at helping someone to look objectively at what they want from their career, what they are getting and how they might change things for the better.

Some of the larger recruitment consultancies claim that they can offer independent advice as well, for which they would not charge the recipient. However, they would not be able to devote the same amounts of time to counselling as a paid specialist, and would always have a vested interest in encouraging the candidate to move jobs, however much they might protest to the contrary.

The quality of the advice on offer depends completely on the quality of individual advisers, and this is such a subjective matter that it is hard to draw up any guidelines by which to judge the firms and the services they are offering.

A lot of the advice is common sense, but candidates need the one-to-one attention to help their morale. It is a difficult process to do for oneself.

Anyone who offers advice can call him- or herself an adviser, whether it is a family solicitor, someone propping up a bar or a five-year-old explaining life to a three-year-old.

Someone who has talked to a professional adviser and has, as a result, improved their working life, is likely to recommend that adviser to other people. Likewise if another person has paid for the service but does not feel that their life has changed in any way, they are going to brand that adviser a charlatan. It may be that the same adviser spoke to both people, that they were successful with one and not the other – it is a question of personal chemistry – but there are some who probably please most of their clients most of the time, and some who do the opposite.

A skilful counsellor can help a candidate to 'lift the blinkers' which tend to grow on anyone who has been doing a job for a long time, and help them to see their positions objectively. They can help you to see your achievements and to see problems that might be coming. They help you to take stock. If, for instance, you have been passed over for a job that you feel should by rights be yours, they can talk it through with you and help you to understand why it happened. It might even be a major event in someone's private life, like losing a spouse, which can trigger them into wanting to take stock of their position and go for counselling. The majority of people will probably never have spent so long actually thinking and talking about themselves, their hopes and fears. It might be the first time they have reviewed their goals since leaving school, or possibly even the first time ever. Most people under-estimate themselves and their abilities, and a skilful counsellor can help to raise their self-esteem.

Counsellors can also advise on specific subjects like interviewing skills, how to prepare for them and how to put oneself across effectively, and how to write successful CVs. It could be that the candidate will end up getting a new job in the process of the counselling, alternatively it might just be an opportunity to review progress, strengthen weaknesses, see which skills need enhancement, and get into better shape for the rat race back at work. In some cases the counsellor might talk a candidate into putting their own employer on to a list of target companies to approach for new jobs.

In the majority of cases the consultants are called in and paid for by the employers in order to help with a personnel problem. It may be an 'outplacement' problem, involving taking a number of people who are being 'phased out' and counselling them on how to raise their morale and go about finding other things to do. Alternatively it might be that an individual within the company is dissatisfied and threatening to leave, and the employers want to find a way of motivating him or her to stay. So they call in a consultant to try to work out with the individual what it is that they want from their careers and how they can go about getting it while remaining with their existing employer.

Although a great proportion of the income that flows into the career advisory industry therefore comes from the corporations there are situations in which an individual might call on a consultant's services and pay for them privately. For the person who is in control of their own destiny but needs someone to talk to, some of the consultants offer a useful service.

Suppose, for whatever reason, you are dissatisfied with your career and the way it is going. It might be that you have reached one of the blockages we talked about earlier, or it might be that you feel you are in the wrong industry but you don't know which would be the right one. It might be that you simply don't think you know enough about how to control your own career and destiny. Perhaps you have a personality clash with your boss and you don't know how to resolve it, or there is a possibility of a promotion in the pipeline and you don't know whether to go for it or not.

What you need most of all in these situations is someone to talk to who will be willing and eager to listen. Someone who is wise in the ways of the career world, who doesn't have a vested interest in persuading you to follow one course or another, and who is willing and able to ask the right questions so that you can discover the right answers for yourself.

There are not many consultants who are that skilled, but there are some. There are also companies that offer open courses on the subject, and a number of other permutations on the same theme. There is a place for all of them.

In an ideal world, employees who feel they have these problems should be able to go to their bosses or their personnel departments and talk it over. No doubt in such circumstances they would be assured that the talk was confidential, but it would be hard for them to dissociate the person they were talking to from the problem. All the time that they could see the personnel manager taking notes as they talked it would be hard for them to believe that their words were really 'off the record'. A career adviser offers an arm's-length service, allowing the individual to relax and un-burden in complete privacy and safety, and giving the company the benefit of a happy and grateful employee.

On the open courses that some companies hold the privacy element is not so apparent. This might make them less attractive to very senior management, but the participants are still safe from the ears of their employers – who may not even know they are there – and they are also able to share their experiences with other people who are searching for ways to improve and enrich their lives and careers.

Many consultants will provide you with value for money if you believe that you need their services. They are not cheap, however, and it is therefore better to go to them during the good times rather than during the bad. If you have just been fired and you are trying to find your way back into the world of work you may resent paying out a four-figure sum to someone who seems in the long run to do little more than talk common sense to you. The fact that you were not able to exercise that common sense without their help may not appear obvious to you at the time you are writing the cheque to cover their fees. If, on the other hand, you go to them when you are fully employed and merely trying to find the most effective way to move forward, you will consider it money well spent provided you end up knowing where you are going and how you are going to get there.

A good consultant will be able to help you to do some lateral thinking. It is possible that you have been heading in the wrong direction for some years. You may have been watching the wrong goal posts, or completely misunderstood the best way to get to them. Do you in fact want to stay in the rat race at all, or **would** you rather be running your own vineyard in the south of **France, for instance?** Are you desperately looking around for your next career **move when** it is right under your nose in your own organization?

The fact that career consultancy is becoming bigger business illustrates that people are now beginning to take the whole question more seriously. Consultants are the main evangelists for the message that it is now up to the individual to take charge of his or her own career, and that the individual now employs the company for as long as it is useful, rather than the other way round.

The best career advisers, the ones who work on a one-to-one basis, are rather like Harley Street specialists. They take the time and the trouble to find out exactly what is wrong with you. By getting you to talk and recognize what is going on in your own life, they are able to discover what is happening underneath the top layer of show which we all put on to get through our daily lives. If you go to a busy personnel manager in your own company you are talking to the equivalent of a general practitioner who has the skill to identify symptoms and the experience to recommend cures for them, but who may not have the time or ability to look more deeply at what has caused the symptoms to occur in the first place and how to ensure that they don't reoccur a few months or years down the line. It is always a bad idea to go for the quick fix if you can afford to do the job more thoroughly.

One of the problems facing all managers in their workplaces is that they believe they have to give the appearance of infallibility, demonstrating all the time that they are sure of what they are doing, and that they have a certainty of purpose about all their decisions. Such an attitude is seen by many people to be one of the fundamental requirements of leadership. Voicing doubts and indecision to colleagues within the work environment is seen as evidence of unthinkable weakness, something which may be held against a manager later on when it comes time for a promotion or a new job description. In the privacy of an adviser's office, however, managers can voice all their fears and doubts, they can test their ideas and assumptions, and if they discover they are talking nonsense it doesn't matter. If they discover that they are talking sense they will go away with renewed confidence in their abilities and increased faith in their future success.

In the competitive working environment self-exposure is often not a good idea, but with a consultant managers can let out all the pent-up steam. They can role play, re-enacting scenes they have had with their bosses, or that they are planning to have. They can break down in tears if that is what is needed, and no one else will ever know about it. Most importantly, they are able to be honest. If the adviser asks them why they have said something, they can answer 'I don't know' – they don't have to think up elaborate justifications for everything they say, as they might if they were talking to their bosses.

Everyone in management circles is talking about the importance of change if companies are to survive, and they all admit that change is a hard concept for many people to handle. It is in the interests of companies to equip their people to be adaptable and flexible enough to cope with whatever changes in working practices are necessary. One way to do this is through effective training, but managers may also need to talk through their own doubts with someone who has the time and the inclination to discuss their strengths and weaknesses, and who can help them to analyse how they should be tackling new jobs and new challenges.

So how do you tell the good advisers from the rest? The answer can only be to go to talk to them and make your own judgements. Are they individuals whose opinions you would normally seek out and respect? How keen do they seem to be to get you to sign on the dotted line and part with some money? The best ones have all the work they need and will not want to take on anyone who isn't certain that they will benefit from the experience.

The career advisory business is in a similar position to the one occupied by the headhunters a decade ago. They have a genuine and valuable service to offer. They are just beginning to establish the marketplace, and the potential need for their services is growing. They do not, however, need to have any great qualifications for setting up, and there are still as many bad ones as good. The good ones, however, are keen to make themselves respected as a profession, and are therefore behaving scrupulously carefully. Seek them out.

32   Crisis management

Things will go wrong in even the most well-organized of careers. People may persuade you into making bad decisions and turning up blind alleys by joining companies that are wrong for you or that are going nowhere themselves. You may even end up being made redundant through no fault of your own. If your employer merges with a company of similar size, for instance, there may only be room for one marketing director, and you may end up drawing the short straw. None of these things need harm a career, provided the mistakes are recognized quickly and handled positively.

Supposing you have started your career well with a good company, and then you are lured away to a smaller company that no one has ever heard of. They have given you a better job title, more money, a stake in the company, and the promise that as the business grows you will be shot to glory. Within a couple of months you realize that you have made a mistake. It may be that the company is going places, but that you just aren't suited to the corporate culture, or it may be that the boss is about to run off with the money, leaving you to face the angry hordes. Either way you have made a genuine mistake and no one will hold that against you; they may even believe that it has been a valuable lesson to you, provided you are open and honest about it, and provided you put the situation right as soon as you realize your mistake.

If, however, you do nothing about it, perhaps telling yourself that things aren't as bad as they seem and that if you just wait a year or two the boss will make good on all the recruitment promises, then you will have demonstrated an inability to assess situations correctly even when you are in the midst of them, and a further inability to act when a problem needs a solution.

It would be harder to explain to someone later why you stayed in an inappropriate company for five years, getting nowhere, than it would be to explain why you left after only six months.

When someone is fired or forced to resign from a company it is all too easy for them to look back with the benefit of hindsight and tell themselves that they saw it coming. The moment the new boss arrived, for instance, they believe they knew they were not going to be able to work together successfully. If it is true that they knew this, then they should have started looking for ways out of the situation the moment they realized they were unhappy with it. Had they started planning their departure from the company then, they could have made it less painful for themselves and for the company, and they would have had time to line up their next opportunity.

This comes back to the 'what if' games that we all need to play at regular intervals. When a new boss arrives you need to ask yourself, 'What if we don't get on? Should I stay and wait for them to go, or should I use it as an opportunity to move onwards and upwards somewhere else?' The day your employers start to cut back the staff in your department, ask yourself whether you honestly believe that they are doing it to make the department fitter and leaner and more able to compete, or whether they are just trimming off people to save money and you may be the next on the list. Always try to anticipate what might happen and know what alternatives are likely to be open to you.

Someone who plans and prepares for their departure from an organization is going to be much more popular with the company they are leaving than someone who stalks off in a sulk, leaving their colleagues to cover for them until a replacement can be found and trained up. It is always important to leave your old company thinking well of you; you may need references in the future, you want them to remain on your network, and you might even want to go back one day when you have strengthened your position in the outside market. Never burn your bridges unless you have to.

The danger for anyone who is made redundant is that they will panic and grab the first job that comes along. While it is important to get straight back into the saddle and not to sit around feeling sorry for yourself and allowing your morale to slip ever lower, it is also important to see a situation like this as an opportunity to move up a rung on the ladder, not as a knock-back. If you were a marketing manager and you have been made redundant, that leaves you free to look for a marketing directorship somewhere else. This is a slightly simplistic way of putting it, but it is important to view the situation positively and to plan your next move carefully.

A crisis like this may be a good time to utilize the services of an outplacement agency at the expense of your former employer, or a career adviser of your own choice, in order to get some professional guidance on how to rebuild your ego and decide in which direction to aim next. Analyse what you have achieved so far and where you want to go next. Don't panic about the lack of money coming in. If you are able and talented you will always be able to get another job sooner or later, and even if you end up spending all your redundancy money and then some of your savings while you are searching for the right break, you will be investing the money in a good cause.

In reality a large percentage of people will at some time or another face the shock of unexpectedly losing their jobs for whatever reason. There is now a whole industry of people who understand the problems such an eventuality can cause. There are also a lot of companies selling services to the vulnerable and unwary which are less than good value, but at least they provide human contact when it is most needed.

Most people react in the same way to losing their job through no fault of their own. They start out by being shocked, hardly able to believe that it is happening. As they accept that it is true, they become angry at the people who have betrayed them and at the world in general. They suffer feelings of loss and emptiness which sap their self-confidence and morale. They lose their sense of direction and identity because they have lost the job that gave them their status. They have also lost a group of friends and colleagues who made up a major part of their lives. At a practical level they have probably also been deprived of a company car and of all the administrative back-up they are used to receiving from secretaries, accountants, office managers and all the rest. If you haven't had to buy your own stationery or printing before, it can come as a nasty shock the first time you have to set out to the shops on your own.

The feelings of rejection and loss of self-esteem make people believe they have failed, that nobody wants them and that they never were any good at their job anyway. This feeling becomes worse as they apply for new jobs and find that the majority of their letters go unanswered, or receive standard notes of rejection.

People in management, who are used to having some degree of control over their lives, suddenly find that they have lost control. Someone else has taken control and forced a change of circumstances on to them. They are suddenly in a position of relying on other people to give them interviews and job offers, where before they could instruct that things should happen and expect results.

On top of that, a redundant manager is likely to be feeling guilty about letting his family down and feeling a sense of shame at the social stigma of being out of work. All these emotions are going on inside at a time when people are having to come to terms with enormous changes in their lives and circumstances. Losing a job is one of the most stressful things that can happen to someone, partly because of the fear of change and uncertainty which is in most of us.

If there are genuine reasons for your dismissal, however, and you keep your head, you will inevitably get another job at the same or even a better salary. If you are in this position because you have made a mistake, then you must face that fact and approach the next stage of your career as positively as you were approaching jobs before it happened. The most important task confronting anyone at times like this is getting back into a job. Any emotional strains that interfere with this task are dangerous and need to be tackled. In most cases the best way to tackle them is to talk to someone else and not to bottle them up.

Whatever mistakes you have made in your career, be honest about them, and learn from them. When you go for future jobs or you are talking to people like headhunters, don't try to gloss over any gaps in your CV, and don't try to dress up the reasons why you left previous employers. An experienced recruiter will see through an old cliché like 'we had a difference of opinion over long-term strategy' in two seconds (if it is true, then you will have to give more detail to demonstrate why you believe your stance was the correct one). If, on the other hand, you explain that you and the boss just didn't get on, or that you made a mistake by going to that company, but you only stayed a year and during that year you learned some valuable lessons, they will be happy to accept it. No one expects a career to be plain sailing all the way; in fact someone who has never made mistakes probably hasn't taken many risks either, and might not be the best person for a senior management position.

If, however, you don't appear to learn by your mistakes, and you continue to repeat them, then future employers are going to start voicing doubts. If you have moved every year or two throughout your career, and each time you blame the company involved, they are soon going to question your judgement, even if they don't start to distrust your word. Everyone is entitled to one or two mistakes, more than that and they will start to count against you.

Times of crisis offer good opportunities for self-evaluation. You need to keep calm and work out what is happening, and what you want to happen in the future. You need to work out which companies you would like to work for and then contact them to let them know you are available and would like to come and talk to them.

Although you don't want to rush into the wrong job, you do want to get the right job as quickly as possible, so you need to approach everyone immediately. Although you should approach every sort of agency and consultancy that offers its services and is within your price range, you should not rely on them getting the jobs for you. You need to rely on your own efforts. You need to be simultaneously answering advertisements, letting headhunters know you are available, writing direct to potential employers and networking. Getting re-employed needs to be treated like a job, starting at nine each morning and ending at five or later in the evening.

If you have been made redundant low morale is going to be your biggest problem, and anyone who can help you overcome that will be worth paying. You may need to go after consulting work as well as full-time jobs to fill in the time before you find the right niche for yourself, this will help you to make new contacts and to keep yourself in the swim.

You need to practise and perfect interview techniques, working on verbal and non-verbal language, confrontational and non-confrontational situations, and all the disciplines needed to make a good impression.

Marketing is not a highly secure profession. Redundancies and sackings are likely to increase as companies ebb and flow, hiring marketing departments in the good years and then laying them off when the next downturn comes. You need to be ready and prepared to sell yourself convincingly the moment that something goes wrong.

Writing a CV

Although a CV should reflect your individual personality and career pattern, there are certain guidelines which help to make them useful and readable to potential employers and help you to get new jobs.

The initial aim of the CV is to get you an interview – to make someone believe that you are worth seeing. This means that before anything else, it needs to be neatly typed and presented, just as you would present yourself at an interview.

Brevity is also a plus point. If you can get the main points on to one side of A4 paper you stand a better chance of holding the reader's attention, and two or three pages should be the maximum length. If you have a long list of qualifications or publications then you could list these on a separate page.

The most important information must be on the first page, because only if you have caught the reader's attention immediately will he or she bother to read on.

Make sure your name, address and telephone number are on the sheet in case it becomes separated from your covering letter, and stick to the facts. Do not try to describe yourself or your achievements in glowing prose. They want to see the bare bones of what you have taken on and what you have achieved; they will make their own value judgements about whether you are 'dynamic' or a 'self-starter' when they meet you. They will not believe that you are these things just because you say so.

Never forget that the CV is a marketing document, and you need to make very clear to readers why they need to buy your services. You need to lay out the reasons for purchase very clearly.

CEPEC, one of the UK's leading outplacement consultants provides a list of contents which they believe should be in a CV. They have re-searched what most employers require and have discovered that they don't want to be sent an applicant's photograph. They want personal details like address and telephone number at the beginning of the CV, not at the end. They want the applicant's nationality to be stated, and a note of the schools attended, even by senior staff.

If you have a proficiency in any other languages you should let them know about it, and also let them know if you are willing to relocate. If there are limits to the distance you would be willing to move they want to know what these are.

They then want to see your last job listed first, with last or current salary and an indication of any other benefits like a car or private health scheme.

You should then briefly state your career aims but not bother to list any of your 'personal characteristics'.

Employers like to see responsibilities and achievements listed against each appointment rather than a table of appointments first, followed by a paragraph of responsibilities and achievements covering a whole career.

They also want to know about your leisure interests under the heading 'Other activities', which will give you an opportunity to mention any activities outside work, either past or present.

They need to know something about the products and the size of the companies you have worked for, and a brief summary of professional, managerial or other principal achievements, provided these are strictly factual.

They do not, at this stage, need a list of referees.

Although respondents to CEPEC's research said that they liked to know an applicant's salary expectations, CEPEC suggests caution in disclosing too much too soon. Salary is an important part of the negotiation for any job. If you are replying to an advertisement which clearly states the salary range on offer, CEPEC suggests that there is no reason to conceal your current earnings, although if they greatly exceed or fall short of the figure shown you will need a convincing explanation for your interest.

When writing speculatively to employers, CEPEC advises that you do not disclose your salary at the first approach. The aim is to interest the employer in you as a potentially valuable addition to the organization, and then to consider your price.

If you are going through recruitment consultancies, they will usually have limited scope to vary the starting salary agreed with the employer, so it is best when applying speculatively for work to tell the consultant your current salary expectations.

Your CV is your sales document, and as such it must sound businesslike and convincing, and present the information in an attractive way.

33 Developing a track record

The further you get up any corporate ladder, the less relevant your original qualifications will become. By the time you have become a managing director of a major company, few people are going to be bothered about whether you started out with a degree or whether you worked your way up from the post of office cleaner. The very fact that you have got so far will indicate that you are able to handle people and convince them of your abilities. Your track record begins to speak for itself.

Everyone, therefore, needs to be keeping an eye on their track record. Nothing is as good a sales aid as a good, checkable track record. Just as you need to stop every so often and take stock of your goals and whether you are still on course for them, you also need to pause and look backwards in your wake, to see what your past is beginning to look like. When you are living life from day to day, tackling each problem as it arises and surviving from crisis to crisis, it is sometimes easy to forget just how much you have achieved in the past, and therefore to be unduly modest in your goals.

It is equally easy to muddle through from one thing to the next and completely fail to build up any sort of record of achievement, even though you have the opportunities for success all around you and to the casual observer you seem to be succeeding. The key word in all this is 'achievement'; you have got to be able to demonstrate it almost from the first year you are employed.

There are certain situations that are particularly useful on a track record, because they show that you are able to achieve measurable results through others. You can't hope to have achieved all of them, but you should certainly seek out as many as you can along the way.

You should have a proven profit-and-loss track record, showing that you understand the bottom line and how to balance and control it.

You should have some experience of turning round a loss-making product or division, to demonstrate that you can work against the odds and still come out on top.

You should have been involved in a successful new product introduction or new market development, to show that you can take calculated risks and think creatively.

Some experience of corporate finance is going to be invaluable to you at later stages, although you could fill this gap with training if necessary.

Above all else, however, you should have a record for developing other people. Someone who can get the best out of a team, and can create promising young executives for the future, is going to be of immense value to any company.

If you keep your eye on these goals you should be able to find situations in almost any company of any size that will provide the right levels of experience. Any company that is good at training its people will move you around every two years or so to stop you getting bored. If you make it known what you would like to do at each move, the chances are that the company will try to accommodate you. It is much harder for small companies to be able to provide this variety of roles, but at the same time senior managers in small companies probably get to cross over between different functions whatever their job titles are.

At the beginning of the book we talked about providing employers with signposts by which to judge what sort of performer you are likely to be in the future. If you have a good university degree and have done interesting things with your spare time, they are going to be able to draw conclusions about the sort of person you are and the sort of contribution you are likely to make to the company. If, however, you fail to achieve any of the goals they set for you, or fail to set any new ones of your own, it will not be long before your early qualifications are worthless. There are plenty of people in the working world who do not have university qualifications, who will be more than happy to see evidence that they are meaningless, and that having a good degree does not mean that you will be a success in the 'real world'. These people will be only too pleased to watch you fail, and shake their heads knowingly.

From the moment you get your first decent job people are going to be looking for signals that you are continuing to succeed, that you are learning and expanding your horizons and that you are achieving tangible results.

In order to build up an impressive track record you are going to have to conform to certain expected career patterns, unless you have a good reason not to. People are going to expect to see you achieving certain stages in your career by certain ages. If you are not keeping to a recognizable pattern, then you are going to have to be able to give a good explanation as to why you are not doing so. There is no reason why everyone should have to follow exactly the same career pattern – in fact it would be ridiculous to expect them to do so – but anyone who hasn't got all the easily understood badges of success will need to have a clear plan that they can demonstrate as being on course, and they will need to be able to point to some solid results.

It might be more impressive for a potential employer, for example, to be able to see that you remained as a brand manager for two years longer than a contemporary who is after the same job, provided the reason that you stayed was in order to see through a product launch from start to finish. That way they know that you are willing to pass up easy glories and were willing to take responsibility for any problems that might have arisen once your original concept became a reality on the shelves of the supermarkets.

Typical high-fliers in large fmcg companies might spend only two years as assistant brand or product managers. They might then spend a further year or two as brand or product managers before moving on to become group product managers or senior brand managers. Six or so years after they started they should be marketing managers, making it to marketing director around ten years from the beginning. During that time it is possible that they have never actually seen a product through from concept to profit. They have never actually taken responsibility for something from beginning to end. Their progression and rate of promotion is excellent, and conforms to all the right patterns, but they may still lack any hard evidence that they are able to run something for themselves and take full responsibility for its success or failure.

In the service industries you might be involved in the creation of a new idea and its launch, and will not then be around to deal with the customer complaints and fine tuning necessary once the product is in the market-place. The same is true in the industrial sector, where the sales cycle for a product might be several years, and it might be three years before the customers actually see some satisfaction.

These fast movers may also not have taken out any time to broaden themselves, by going into sales, or consultancy, or any of the marketing services along the way. Although they may have been involved with some blue-chip products and all the various pieces of the marketing jig-saw, they may not actually have acquired many technical skills of their own. It might be that someone who has taken it a little slower, but learned the business more thoroughly, might be a better bet to an employer after ten years, than someone who has flown straight to the top. Once again it is a question of the strength of the roots and the trunks of the trees, as opposed to the spread of the branches.

The same problem can occur with too many moves between companies. It is all very well having a list of the best blue-chip names that you have worked for, having changed horses every two years of your career, but the question arises again as to whether you have actually been in any one place long enough to take responsibility for your own actions.

At the same time, if you have stayed in one company for ten years, potential employers might question whether you would easily be able to move to a new culture, and whether your experience of life has been broad enough. Two jobs each of five years' duration might be close to the ideal track record by that stage, but every case is different. There might be excellent reasons why you have stayed with one company, and even, possibly, equally good reasons for moving every two years.

Whenever you are not suitable for a job or promotion that you really wanted, people are going to suggest that it is one of these factors that is responsible for holding you back, and the same people may be giving completely contradictory advice to someone else. There is no ideal blueprint for everyone to follow.

The only way to build a track record is to gain results, and there are many different ways of doing that. It means being involved with the right projects at the right times, and being able to explain to people why your contribution made a difference. It might be better to miss a promotion in your company's head office but to accept an offer to set up a distribution network for them in a new territory, something that you can make succeed and claim the glory as your own. It might be better to miss out on a routine salary increase, but accept a project to take an ailing brand and turn it round. Simply having grand titles and large salaries will not be enough to convince people that you are worth employing. Sooner or later you will be found out. But if you have an unassailable record of achievement, no one can argue, apart from which you will also have trained yourself in how to build a business for yourself. Once you have that ability you no longer need your employers as much as they need you, and that gives you all the power.

34 *Into general management*

So now you are within sight of a managing directorship. The first question to ask yourself at this stage is 'Do I really want to make this final jump?'

The higher up the corporate ladder you climb the less satisfaction you are likely to be able to get from actually getting a job done well, and the more time you are going to have to spend on political problems and general administration tasks. You are going to be split between a wide range of tasks, from determining the strategic direction of the organization to developing team work and promoting the business. Do you truly believe you are the sort of personality that will thrive on this sort of pressure?

There will be a lot of satisfactions along the way, from both individual and team actions, but there will also be a lot of frustrations brought about by people and events beyond your control. The danger for people who are used actually to 'doing things' rather than 'managing things' is that they yearn to be back at the coal-face, and end up interfering with the work their subordinates are doing, instead of managing them.

For some people, to become number one in a company is their ultimate goal, and it is the political struggles they thrive on, both on the way up and once they get there. They have used marketing as the best way to get to the top, and do not have any particular love for the profession. These people will have been taking care to gain general management experience along the way. They will have been on the right courses, perhaps including an MBA, and they will have made sure that they acquired the right track record, becoming known and recognized for getting results and being able to see the broader picture.

Research in America has shown that only 25 per cent of the people who start out in marketing are still in the same sector when they reach the top of their careers, against 64 per cent who start in finance or accounting. Marketing is generally used as a way to gain a broad grounding in business from which to move on to other things. If a company is marketing led, there will always be ways of moving into general management from the marketing department.

The major question these people will have to ask themselves is how quickly they want to get to a position of ultimate power. Would they, for instance, rather go to a smaller company on their way up, and be involved in making it grow, which might mean that they could become chief executives in their early thirties? Or would it be better in the long term to serve a longer apprenticeship in a major company, in the hope of getting to the top job there, perhaps in their forties or possibly even later?

There are risks in either decision. If you go with a small company there is a possibility the company might fail, through no fault of yours, and you will be left with a major blemish on your track record. If you stay on with the large company you might realize as you get towards fifty that you are not actually going to get to the top job, and by then it might be too late to break away and do something else. By that stage you will probably have grown too used to the comforts of a large organization to be able to take the plunge into the outside world. You will also be getting close to your pension and may not be able to justify losing the last set of bonuses. You may not even be as attractive to other employers now that it is obvious that you want to move because you have failed to get where you want in your first choice of company.

For those who move to smaller companies in order to climb further up the corporate ladder, there is the added problem of suddenly finding themselves isolated from the corporate machine. If you are used to having a huge back-up team all around you, you may feel very naked if suddenly you are making all the decisions yourself.

It might be that a few years spent building up a small company in your thirties would be a good training ground for moving back into a blue-chip organization later, perhaps when the blue-chip buys your company out, giving you some capital and a senior position in the parent company. Anyone who stays with a large company from start to finish is going to have to resign themselves to always having to rely on their salaries for their income, with little chance of building capital unless an opportunity arises for a management buy-out of their department. You need to be sure that you have the necessary entrepreneurial fire in your belly before embarking on these types of exercise, however, otherwise you may find that the strains of general management ruin both your health and your peace of mind.

The majority of people do not have their ultimate goals in mind when they first set out on their careers. In fact most of them set out with no goals at all, which is why they do not get very far.

It is more usual for someone of twenty to know roughly where they want to be by thirty and then to continue looking ahead in five- to ten-year bites. Under those circumstances the majority of marketing people do not see their profession as a stepping stone to anything else but as an end in itself, and they are quite happy to be doing what they are doing at every level. These are the people who succeed at their jobs because they concentrate on doing them well, and they are also the people who are offered the opportunities to move on to greater glories.

When the opportunity to move into general management arises – as will be the case with increasing frequency as marketing becomes more established as a recognized route to top management – the candidates have to do some serious thinking. They are probably very good at their current jobs, otherwise people would not be considering them for a promotion. So do they want to risk moving on to something that might prove to be beyond their capabilities? Alternatively, do they want to risk turning down an opportunity that might not present itself again?

It is common for major organizations to plan for succession, and to provide opportunities for learning and being tested. One of the things that needs to be evident is the ability to motivate others, including those with unfamiliar disciplines and special roles.

The decision will be easier if at some stage of your career path you have spent some time in other departments of the company. Whether it is finance, personnel or other management functions doesn't matter, so long as you were able to get an outside view of marketing for a time and a broader perspective on business in general. That way you will be more able to assess whether you would be happy to move out of the marketing stream once and for all, or whether you would miss being at the sharp end of the business day-in and day-out.

In some cases a move into general management might actually be a way of slowing down. If you are currently group marketing director of one of the big blue-chip companies, with a job that involves a lot of travel and pressure, you might find that the managing directorship of a small manufacturer in the same sector would not only pay better and offer the chance of building something, but would actually be a less pressured environment. A good managing director, who is skilled at delegating and able to attract the best people, will have far more time for reflection and strategic thinking than a hard-pressed marketing director.

This may, then, be a job more suited to someone of maturer years than a marketing directorship in a high pressure company. On the other hand, to take on a managing directorship of a company that is in a declining sector and in need of turning round could be a nightmare that someone who has a comfortable job within a company they are confident will survive at least into the forseeable future may not need.

There is also a degree of timing involved, linked to the overall trends of the business world. If, for instance, your sector of the business world is in an expansive mood, it will favour managers who are good at business building and motivating people to grow. That is a skill good marketing people should have in abundance. If, on the other hand, there is an air of recession, it might be a time more suited to managers who can tighten belts and prune companies back to survive through lean times. The successful managers during these periods are more likely to come from finance, where the skills of control and survival are more important than those of growth.

If marketing people are to make themselves indispensable when the going gets tough, they need to be able to operate in all climates, not just those of boom and growth. The problem is to give marketing people the training and experience in management while they are on their way up. This is particularly difficult outside large marketing departments.

A great marketing person who comes to the fore at a time like the early 1980s may be able to lead a company to great achievements, and there are plenty of examples of people who did just that. When the boom period ends, as it did in the retail sector at the end of the 1980s, these people suddenly begin to look too extravagant and too flamboyant. They become anachronisms almost over-night and the media and investors who so happily built them up as heroes while things were going well are just as happy to knock them down as villains when the tide turns. People who were being fêted for their brilliant, optimistic strategies of growth are suddenly criticized for their hype and their lack of caution. As a result they cannot go down in the final analysis as 'great' managers.

Anyone thinking of moving into general management should seriously consider whether their abilities and skills fit in with the mood of the times. If the answer is no, it might be wiser to wait until they do. There are, however, always going to be ups and downs in the business cycle, and the good managing director is the one who can operate in both situations. The greatest secret of successful management is probably to choose your advisers wisely.

35 *Playing the political games*

It is easy to become unduly cynical about the part office politics play in whether someone succeeds or fails in their career, but there is certainly a strong element of it in everyone's working life.

Just as a recruit to a company has to be sure that they can fit comfortably into the company culture, they have also got to be sure that they will be comfortable with the people around them, both alongside and above.

When a sample of redundancies was analysed recently, the one common factor found between them was political naïvety. Often the free thinkers and bright sparks of a company are so busy beavering away at their jobs that they ignore company politics and the art of self-marketing, ending up being the scapegoats for other people's mistakes.

One man in the sample, when trying to analyse why he had lost his job, admitted that most of the people in the company went to the pub after work. He didn't like pubs and because he had a long drive home he never joined them. As a result he became isolated and couldn't relate to his boss. He heard later that the seemingly informal meetings at the bar were actually the places where a lot of the company's business was being talked about. By not joining in, he had rejected his boss and his peer group and had gained a reputation for being difficult and uncooperative.

Anyone joining a company and hoping to be successful must recognize the politics that are in action. If they then say they 'won't play', they are likely to be the losers. Being good at a job is not enough; you need to be good with people and part of a team if you are going to get to the top in corporate life. You must therefore choose a team with which you want to play and in which you think your talents will be appreciated. The greatest football player in the world would soon be destroyed by joining a third-division team.

The moment you decide to take charge of your career you have become a political animal. The capacity for politics is born in most of us; whether or not we realize this depends on our life's experiences, and those experiences will depend on the choices we make.

Good company people are always happy to work as members of teams relating easily to colleagues. There are also those who have 'self employed' mentalities but realize that they need to get inside the big companies in order to succeed. The latter group will give their employers good value because they are guarding their own careers. If a company can recognize them and treat them right, it can keep them.

The most important thing to have while you are on your way up is a mentor, someone who is a layer or two above you, and who looks as if they are going places. If you are recruited into a company by someone who likes you, and they grow to like and respect you more as they work with you, the chances are that when they are promoted to a bigger and better job, they will want to take you with them. You will have become as much part of their network as they are part of yours. People like to work with those they know and trust.

The cold-blooded question you have to ask yourself is whether the person who is your mentor is going to go to the top. It could be a very bad move to be taken on by someone who is obviously your inferior when it comes to ability. It might seem a good idea at the time, because you imagine yourself being able to overtake them very quickly, but the chances are that as soon as you begin to show how good you are, they are going to start to look for ways to slow you down. Who wants to be shown up by their juniors? You would be much better to hang on to the coat tails of someone who is much better than you, if you can find such a person.

If, for instance, you manage to attach yourself to someone who is a future managing director, that could mean you have a clear path to a marketing directorship by staying at their side. The problem might then come when it was time for you to take the final jump and the only person standing between you and the top job is the friend and colleague to whom you owe your whole success. Are you then going to try to take their job from them, or are you going to desert them and move on to pastures new? It could be a painful decision either way.

Some people find office politics virtually impossible to cope with. They may be excellent at their jobs, but they just can't bring themselves to join in with the undignified jostling for position that goes on in any company. These people, who probably have attitudes more akin to the self-employed fraternity, are still able to thrive in big company atmospheres simply because they have automatically grasped the rules of controlling their own destinies. These people do not feel any obligation to devote their lives to a company or to a team of any sort, they merely stay for as long as the relationship is mutually beneficial. As soon as it stops being so, they start to look around for something that will fit their needs more exactly.

This is precisely the sort of attitude which will grow and multiply as more companies devolve and move into using freelance specialists for more functions. Those who choose to remain within the frameworks of corporate structures will become more used to the idea of working for themselves, and hiring out their services to their employers on a contract basis. It will alter the nature of office politics considerably, but it will never eradicate them.

36   *The third age*

By the age of fifty-five you are still only two-thirds of the way through your useful working life. If you were a great entrepreneur or a cabinet minister you would probably just be reaching the peak of your powers. Yet the vast majority of managers at this age start to talk about retiring, and have visions of not having to struggle any more for a living. They think they will be able to devote themselves to their homes, their hobbies and their grandchildren, and live happily without the trials of commuting, making presentations and attending to the bottom line. To do so may prove to be a sad waste of opportunities for personal enjoyment and job satisfaction.

Demographic changes, with an increase in older people and a decrease in younger ones, make it more important now that no one is encouraged to mentally retire at fifty-five.

Some of the people who take the traditional 'retirement' path are able to lead perfectly happy and fulfilled lives, as integral and much needed parts of their families and communities. When others do it, however, they cut themselves off from all that has gone before in their working lives virtually over-night, and they wither and die from the resulting lack of stimulation. Once they have done whatever they wanted to do to improve their houses and gardens, and have been on a world cruise, they suddenly realize that they need more to satisfy themselves.

If they have planned and prepared themselves for this period, then it will be the time during which they can reap the rewards of all their past efforts. If they haven't planned it right, they may find that they are on the scrap heap and unable to do anything beyond the anachronistic stereotyping assigned to them for their 'retirement'.

There is a growing trend towards thinking in terms of developing a 'retirement portfolio'. This means building up a variety of different things to do, each of which will take up a part of your time and offer different rewards.

For the real high fliers it is not difficult to find projects with which to fill a portfolio. If you have ended your career as a cabinet minister or the chairman of a multinational compay, there are going to be people queuing up to offer you non-executive directorships and consultancy assignments, not to mention the chairmanship of voluntary organizations, and offers from publishers for your memoirs.

If, however, you are a marketing director or manager from a successful company, you will have to think more carefully about what you are going to be able to do, and you will need to prepare and train as you would for any other new challenge. In some cases you may be able to persuade your company to let you go out for a year or two towards the end of your career, on secondment, perhaps to a voluntary organization. That way the company is able to clear the path for other people coming up the career ladder within the company, as well as doing something helpful for you and the community – both of which will be useful public relations exercises. If the company simply pushes you aside because you are in the way and no longer sufficiently useful, people will notice and its reputation will suffer. Likewise it will usually be willing to offer training courses and seminars in how to approach the next stage of your career. Take everything that is on offer, and spend as much time as possible thinking and planning what you are going to do.

The basis of your whole career structure at this stage will be your pension, or pay-off, whichever you have received. Unless you have managed to build up enough money so that your basic, everyday needs are catered for without you having to worry, it is going to be hard to find the energy or optimism to go out in search of new horizons.

Presuming, therefore, that your mortgage is paid off, your children are off your hands, and you have enough of a pension or capital sum to survive at the level at which you are accustomed, you can now begin to think clearly about what it is you want to do with the next stage of your life. You have some very valuable assets in the form of wisdom and experience which you can now sell or give away as you choose.

The first thing that most people in this position will consider is consultancy work. They may offer their services to a consultancy or to their previous employers on a part-time basis, or they might consider setting up in business on their own, with the aim of working two or three days a week. In reality this does not work for the majority of people. The consultancy world is competitive enough for those who are devoting all their energies to it, and who are willing to go anywhere and do anything just to get their businesses off the ground, let alone for someone who wants to treat it as a hobby.

Those whose track records are exceptional, however, and who have a natural gift for consulting, will find that there is an increasing need for consultants who have a long and varied experience to draw from. It might be that someone who retires from a blue-chip company at the age of fifty-five, with an impeccable track record, will be able to walk into a top job at an established consultancy, and will go on to attain ever greater heights in their career. These are the real high fliers.

Most people of this age do not have the stamina or the wish to devote themselves so whole-heartedly to a new career challenge, particularly in such a competitive and demanding sector. While it may be possible, then, to find some part-time consulting work for a while, most people will soon find that their services are less in demand as they grow further away from the jobs that first made their advice useful. If you retired from a top marketing job last year you will have a great deal to contribute to other companies. If you retired from it seven years ago your credibility might not be quite so strong. Once away from the full-time working environment, people sometimes develop a broader perspective on life, begin to see that there is more to happiness than can be offered within the traditional career structure, and feel less inclined to compete with those younger and more blinkered than themselves. Once this attitude takes hold, the work soon begins to dwindle away. Rather than pursue it anxiously, however, they begin to look elsewhere for their job satisfactions. They don't, after all, need the money.

If you want to make consultancy work the main platform for your portfolio at this stage, then you will need to lay some foundations while you are still within the traditional career structure. It will help if you manage to get some consulting experience under your belt as you go along, even if you are not planning to come back to it for a number of years. It will also help if you have made contacts and built a network of people who will be useful when you come to offer yourself to the market. Part of this will be to do with building a reputation in the way we talked about earlier. Someone who has managed to become famous for being able to write and talk about their subject will be able to remain 'saleable' for a good many years after they have left the job that made them famous in the first place.

The people who are most successful in this arena are generally the ones for whom the whole idea of retirement in anathema. For the majority of people coming into the third age, consulting work does not turn out to be as easy or as pleasant as they had imagined, and they soon begin to wind it down and look for other ways to utilize their hard-won skills.

This is where the voluntary sector comes into play and begins to appeal to people who would never have considered giving away their skills in the past. Once someone has got used to the idea of living on a fixed income, and finds that it is not as uncomfortable as they first thought, they begin to think about finding work that provides job satisfaction first and material reward second. They may like to think that they will be able to get some money for their services, but once they begin to look into the market they see that the overwhelming demand comes from organizations that can pay no more than expenses.

As they approach the beginning of their retirement, those who want to go on working should contact organizations that supply skilled personnel to the voluntary sector, just to find out what sort of things would be available to them, so that they can think in advance about how to balance their portfolio.

Anyone who has had experience of marketing and general management can find a niche in the administration of any number of voluntary operations. Marketing people are also naturals at fundraising, a function desperately needed by something like a quarter of a million organizations in Britain at the moment. Although initially senior managers might recoil at the idea, seeing visions of themselves shaking collecting tins in shopping precincts on Saturday mornings, it doesn't take much thought to bring the realization that any voluntary organization in search of funds has to market itself in just the same way as a commercial operation. The people with the collecting tins are simply part of the equivalent of the sales promotion and point-of-sale exercises an fmcg company might devise.

It could be anything from a senior post at Oxfam to the financing of a local children's club; it could be the running of an inner-city programme for drug offenders, to a job with the National Trust or some other equally genteel organization. The need for skilled people is massive, and the potential job satisfaction is equally enormous. It might involve a one-off fundraising project or it might be an ongoing job for as long as the incumbent wanted to stay there.

For many, it is something of a culture shock to move from the corporate sector, where they are accustomed to having their instructions carried out virtually unquestioned, to a voluntary organization where most of the fellow workers are deeply suspicious of the very concept of professionalism, but thousands are beginning to make the jump.

Once someone has a few days of paid work, whether with their old employer, consulting, or doing something completely different from part-time gardening to mini-cabbing, the next thing many of them look for is a voluntary body which could use their services for another couple of days.

37   Case studies

The industrial marketing man

Tom Brannan is an account director and board director at Primary Contact, a business-to-business advertising agency within the Ogilvy and Mather Group.

He started his career with a business degree from Strathclyde University and was offered two jobs on graduation. One was with Marks and Spencer as a trainee manager, the other was with Brown Brothers Ltd, a wholesaler working in several areas of industry. He had little idea of where he wanted to go apart from wanting to gain a broad base in business with a view to getting involved in marketing at some stage.

The Marks and Spencer offer was very tempting, with more money than Brown Brothers were offering, but Tom decided to join Brown Brothers, since he believed that a smaller company would give him more 'hands-on' experience and allow him the opportunity to 'shine' much earlier on. It proved a good move.

Eight months into his eighteen-month graduate training programme they promoted him, and sent him to Edinburgh as a department manager with half a dozen staff under him. It was a major department within the company and Tom was able to prove himself immediately by doubling its turnover.

From there he moved to Black and Decker and into export marketing, selling in particular to eastern Europe. This was his introduction to the international scene which was to lead him eventually to selling in over sixty different countries and becoming fluent in both French and German.

He moved from Black and Decker to Hestair Eagle, a specialist vehicle body builder, and spent five years selling overseas for them. He began to become involved in marketing as well.

His next job was as sales and marketing director for another specialist vehicle bodywork builder called Shelvoke and Drewry, and he turned the company round from a loss to a profit in two years.

From there he moved on to Lancer Boss, the forklift truck manufacturers, as marketing director. Although it is a large firm, Lancer Boss is privately owned by a family who keep a firm control, and Tom decided that there was not going to be room for him as an outsider at the top of the company.

Primary Contact was the company's advertising agency, and when he mentioned his restlessness to the agency boss they offered him a job on the spot.

Although he intended to stay in the agency world for a couple of years, seeing it as a way to broaden his experience, Tom is still there six years later, enjoying the variety of work. He spends his time working on strategic marketing plans with his clients, who vary from agri-chemical companies to the fashion industry to major capital goods manufacturers, and his team then takes on the implementation work. Being able to talk authoritatively on international markets is a considerable asset.

If he were to give two pieces of advice to beginners in the industry it would be to gain selling experience in order to be able to break down the barriers between marketing and selling at a later date, and to try to get some international experience, ideally with a second language, in order to demonstrate an internationalistic attitude.

Woman at the top

Lorna Winstanley studied sociology at Manchester University and graduated in 1968. She had a vague idea in her mind that she wanted to be a researcher of some sort, but had no strategic career plans.

After a number of interviews, and job offers, with blue-chip companies, she accepted an offer from Unilever, partly because they were paying the most money, but partly because they were well known for their training systems and for being a good starting place. Lorna thought their system of employee selection was the most professional she had come across, and the same high standards seemed to permeate throughout the company.

She joined their in-house research compay (RBL) and started work on the whole range of Unilever products from companies like Lever Brothers and Gibbs. She was designing surveys, analysing data, working with computers, presenting to clients and administrating. She was also introduced to 'qualitative research' involving in-depth interviewing of people, which she found she enjoyed.

She saw herself as a market researcher, but the detailed demands of the work, which was then at a pioneering stage with Unilever at the forefront, left her little time to study the other parts of the marketing mix. She did, however, gain a good insight into how research fitted into the overall picture.

After two and a half years she married a Unilever marketing manager. They decided that it would be a wise career move for both of them to move on to something new. Two years, they believed, was the best length of time to stay anywhere.

They both went to Unigate, which was then just changing from being a sleepy, old-fashioned company, into the dynamic, marketing giant we know today. They were part of the marketing team that led the change.

After six months Lorna was in charge of the market research department, doing everything including consumer research and sales analysis. Here, however, she was in the position of buying the research from outside, and she had become part of the management team.

It was an exciting time. The company was launching a number of new products. European interventions were creating things like the butter mountain, which companies like Unigate were trying to market with a host of new product ideas, and chilled cabinets were coming into the supermarkets for the first time, opening up more new marketing possibilities. Cow and Gate, and Bowyers both became part of the company in the three and a half years that Lorna was there.

. In 1973 she had her first child, but continued to work part-time. Her husband moved on again to a job in Brussels and she followed him. Having no particular career plans of her own at the time, she was happy to enjoy her baby and to learn French, something that was to be a boon to her later. She wasn't worried about dropping out since she felt she had gone far enough and had acquired skills which were in demand, so that she could come back into the employment market whenever she chose.

After eighteen months they returned to Derby in England and Lorna took some part-time, freelance work for a local advertising agency as a researcher, as well as doing some industrial market research. She also taught at a local college.

Her husband then decided to change professions and they had an urgent need of a second income. Lorna looked around at the companies in the area, of which there weren't many, and approached Allied Breweries. She was right about her skills being in demand, and they took her on as their research manager, with a huge budget and an important part to play in the marketing team.

At Allied Breweries she was the only woman in senior management, and she found that she kept bumping against 'glass ceilings' which stopped her from moving up as fast as her abilities merited. Although they offered her a job as a marketing manager she declined, believing that she had accrued so much experience and so many contacts as a researcher that she would be wasting her experience if she changed horses at that stage. She would, however, have been happy to move up into a corporate strategic planning role, but there was none available.

By then she had two children and was divorced, and was finding life lonely, so she began to think about moving back down to London. Being based in Derby made it hard to investigate the market thoroughly, but she visited a headhunter who put a number of people in touch with her. Her skills were highly saleable but she didn't feel brave enough at the time to take any risks in her choice of move, and she went to another market research company caled The Qualitative Consultancy.

She enjoyed the work. During her 'fallow period' as a wife and mother she had taken a number of inter-personal training courses for her own amusement, and now found these skills extremely useful. She became a director, and the research industry boomed around her.

The company was owned by a parent company, Aidcom, and there were political disagreements which led Lorna into setting up her own consultancy in partnership with Patsy Douglas who was working with her at the time.

On a rainy Monday morning they set up for business in Patsy's dining room, and five years later they were billing just under a million pounds a year, and deliberately keeping the company's growth rate down in order to concentrate on supplying a quality service and maintaining profitability. The company is now called Winstanley Douglas and Grantham.

Lorna believes that anyone thinking of going into marketing should get as much work experience as possible at the beginning in any marketing-related field they can, in order to see what they are letting themselves in for. Whereas, she believes, many people outside the business world see it as humdrum and faceless, it is actually highly stimulating and involving. She advises talking to as many people as possible, since you can't get a feel of the world of marketing just from reading books. She says she is suspicious of people with marketing degrees since they often seem to lack imagination, creative or writing skills, and are not trained in lateral thinking to the degree that is needed by consultancies like hers.

She is doubtful about the possibilities of planning your career very far ahead, since opportunities will present themselves along the way which will cause you to change direction unexpectedly.

Her career is certainly a good illustration of how to adapt to changing circumstances and to take advantage of opportunities as they arise. The reason that Lorna has been so successful, however, is that she chose to specialize in a skill that is enormously valuable to modern companies. Had she pursued a more general marketing management role, it would have been harder to move around as much as she did at the beginning and maintain her credibility, and virtually impossible to come back into the world of full-time employment at such a high level after having the children.

The need for market research is increasing all the time as companies become more competitive and consumers become more choosy about what they buy.

She advises anyone to get a skill like hers in research or in the high technology fields, and to gain personal skills through training and experience, since 'getting on with people' is going to be one of the most important attributes for someone going into management during the next ten years. She is also a strong supporter of the idea of learning a second language.

The profit-centre man

Anthony Nevile has followed almost none of the prescribed paths in developing his career, and his success demonstrates that if you have the innate ability to succeed, coupled with the energy and personality needed to get the jobs and then to see them through, a formal background is unnecessary.

Anthony was brought up in India and chose National Service rather than university as his first adult learning experience. When he came out of the services he went into industry, starting as a personnel officer at Ford, and modestly claims that he soon discovered he was not a corporate man.

What he succeeded in doing, however, was getting himself put in charge of a number of profit centres in blue-chip companies like Ford, Bowaters and Warner Lambert. He demonstrated an all-round ability to manage the financial and marketing aspects of companies and to see ways of turning them round.

It was Warner Lambert, a heavily marketing-orientated company, which moved him into marketing, and he soon realized that this was where the decisions and the money were made. He began then to look to the future and deliberately set about building a reputation for being able to manage profit centres through marketing, with profit-sharing arrangements which would set him up financially.

Deciding at thirty-five that he was beginning to repeat himself, and not wishing to continue doing the same things for another twenty years, he made a move into consultancy, joining the major accountancy firm Deloittes and doing marketing, financial and strategic work for clients.

He soon realized that he should be working for himself and he moved into the headhunting and consulting business, setting up Anthony Nevile International, which supplies non-executive board directors for major companies all over the world, with offices in England, Munich, Dubai, Singapore, Los Angeles, Baltimore and Tokyo. They specialize in the fmcg, high technology, banking, finance and leisure sectors.

Although Anthony has no qualifications at all, he insists that all the people he hires have the relevant degrees and business qualifications. He also insists that they have worked overseas and been responsible for profit centres.

He sees himself as a 'streetfighter' who has managed to build up a 'credibility bank' by achieving successes for clients either through headhunting, financial or marketing advice, a bank from which he is now able to make withdrawals.

The corporate communications man

At the age of thirty-two, eight years after leaving university, Roy Sully was corporate communications manager for Royal Life Insurance, in charge of the company's corporate identity and corporate advertising. His first job with the company was selling to intermediaries.

It wasn't a strategic career decision, it was simply a job opportunity. The financial services industry was just beginning to take off at the beginning of the 1980s, offering a great deal of scope for young graduates wanting to carve a niche for themselves.

Roy felt that the job bought him time, allowing him to look around and decide what he really wanted to do. It also bought him a satisfying lifestyle in the material sense, and a great deal of freedom, but he felt that the focus was too narrow to be able to satisfy him forever. He began to want a greater challenge.

Having little or no idea what it entailed, he applied for a job as senior marketing assistant at the company's head office, and got it. They were very keen to bring in people who had sales experience, to provide a contrast to the managers who had always worked at the centre of the company and never at the 'sharp end'. His responsibilities included producing sales support material, providing marketing services, copy-writing and dealing with enquiries.

It opened his eyes to the organization as a whole and although he valued the practice he was receiving he felt that the company was moving in the wrong direction, being too sales driven. They were still creating products and then trying to sell them to customers rather than marketing properly.

Of all the aspects of his job, he found the public relations one of the most interesting, and he applied to move down to group head office in London as a press officer. Again his wish was granted, the company being large enough to be able to accommodate most reasonable requests from staff who know what they want to do.

It was only a small department at that stage (1985), but it covered a broad range of activities, particularly dealing with enquiries, reactive telephone work and the production of corporate documents like the anual report and accounts. Roy also edited a worldwide in-house magazine and provided advice and support for the various operating companies.

After a year and a half the group set up their Life Company and he was invited to go back from group head office to Royal Life Holdings, where he was given what he describes as a 'rag-bag of activities'. He was respon-sible for the promotion of the company, press relations, and product promotion. He worked hard to persuade the company of the need to be more open. He became involved in political lobbying and set up a public affairs department. By this stage he was reporting to the corporate marketing manager, who reported directly to the board.

His boss then left and he was able to step into his shoes, introducing a range of marketing practices into the company from product branding to sponsorship and the broader areas of marketing.

Roy believes that his success has been faster because he chose the insurance industry which was a latecomer to marketing. Many of the challenges he was faced with had no precedent within the group and so he was forced to do a great deal of thinking on his feet, having no previous case histories to refer to.

At each stage of his rise he has undertaken specific skills training courses. He believes, however, that the majority of what he knows has been learnt 'on the job', and that one of the most important ingredients for success is choosing the right mentors. He claims that before taking any job he has always taken into account the person who will be above him, and judged whether they have brains which are worth picking and if they are likely to want to share their knowledge with him. He sees marketing as a trade rather than a profession, better learnt from experience than from a book.

His advice to anyone on their way up is to become good at one or two things rather than attempting to master the whole subject of marketing. He believes that sales is a good place to start, since everything you subsequently attempt in marketing will always impact on the sales force in the end.

Although he believes that ultimately it would be logical for him to move into general management, he does not believe that he is ready to make the jump yet. He feels that having been in one industry all his career, he needs to get some alternative company experience before he can make the next step up the ladder. He also confesses that it would be nice to work on some products with more intrinsic appeal than insurance policies.

From journalism to consumer public relations

When Michelle Sammonds left college after training as a journalist, she went straight to work on local papers in the Devon area. After several jobs at the local level she moved to London and worked as a freelance news reporter for papers like the *Daily Mail* and *Mail on Sunday*, before deciding that she wanted to try something different.

'I had had experience of dealing with bad press officers as a journalist,' she remembers, 'and of readng a lot of very badly written press releases, and I was sure I could do better than that.'

She approached a couple of recruitment agencies, one of whom found her a job with public relations consultancy AGB Communications.

'It was a team of fifteen people,' she says, 'working on clients like Birds Eye. In the first six months I thought I had made a mistake. The whole public relations industry seemed to me to be very hysterical and somewhat dishonest. We seemed to have to be unnaturally polite and false to clients and I wasn't comfortable.'

She did, however, enjoy being able to plan and create strategies for the clients, and she enjoyed the opportunities public relations offered for being able to get to know about client companies in depth. Whereas in journalism she had always had to move on to a new story just as she was getting interested in something, public relations allowed her to go deeper into the subjects.

After eighteen months at AGB she moved to Daniel J Edelman, one of the giants of the public relations world, and started work on business-to-business accounts.

'Within a month I could see that it was a mistake,' she admits, 'because some of the accounts were quite technical and I really didn't understand it all. I went to my boss and told him I thought I had come to the wrong place and he suggested I move to the corporate division where I would be looking after clients like the Samaritans, Whyte and Mackay Whisky, and a design consultancy.'

After two and a half years in this job she was approached by W H Smith to work in their in-house public relations department.

'At first it sounded like a really boring name to work for,' she remembers, 'but once I got to the interview I realized just how much potential the company had.'

She started by working on their retail and travel business and is now, at the age of 33, their PR consumer manager, working in a department of twenty-five people, with responsibility for four of their commercial stationery companies. Do-it-All, Our Price and Waterstones.

'Working in-house is more satisfactory than working for a consultancy,' she says, 'because in a consultancy public relations is the be-all and end-all, whereas when you are in-house you are more involved in the total marketing operation. The client company is also more willing to send its people on marketing courses, where consultancies can't afford to spare the time.'

Although she has been on several marketing courses since joining Smiths, Michelle has no concrete plans to move on from public relations.

'I always seem to have just tripped into situations,' she says. 'I am a great believer in the idea that given a basic level of competence you can get whatever you want if you go after it. I would not say that I am a career-orientated person.'

Index